The Essential CALVIN AND HOBBES

A Calvin and Hobbes Treasury

Bill Watterson

Andrews and McMeel A Universal Press Syndicate Company Kansas City

Foreword

Bill Watterson draws wonderful bedside tables. I admire that. He also draws great water splashes and living room couches and chairs and lamps and yawns and screams, and all the things that make a comic strip fun to look at. I like the thin little arms on Calvin and his shoes that look like dinner rolls.

Drawing in a comic strip is infinitely more important than we may think, for our medium must compete with other entertainments, and if a cartoonist does nothing more than illustrate a joke, he or she is going to lose.

Calvin and Hobbes, however, contains hilarious pictures that cannot be duplicated in other mediums. In short, it is fun to look at, and that is what has made Bill's work such an admirable success.

— CHARLES M. SCHULZ

To Tom

A NAUSEOUS NOCTURNE

Another night deprived of slumber,
Hours passing without number,
My eyes trace 'round the room.   I lay

Dripping sweat and now quite certain
That tonight the final curtain
Drops upon my short life's precious play.

From the darkness, by the closet
Comes a noise, much like a faucet
Makes: a madd'ning drip-drip-dripping sound.

It seems some ill-proportioned beast,
Anticipating me deceased,
Is drooling poison puddles on the ground.

A can of Mace, a forty-five,
Is all I'd need to stay alive,
But no weapon lies within my sight.

Oh my gosh! A shadow's creeping,
Ominous and black, it's seeping
Slowly 'cross a moonlit square of light!

Suddenly a floorboard creak
Announces the bloodsucking freak
Is here to steal my future years away!
A sulf'rous smell now fills the room
Heralding my imm'nent doom!
A fang gleams in the dark and murky gray!

Oh, blood-red eyes and tentacles!
Throbbing, pulsing ventricles!
Mucus-oozing pores and frightful claws!

Worse, in terms of outright scariness,
Are the suckers multifarious
That grab and force you in its mighty jaws!

This disgusting aberration
Of nature needs no motivation
To devour helpless children in their beds.
Relishing despairing moans,
It chews kids up and sucks their bones,
And dissolves inside its mouth their li'l heads!

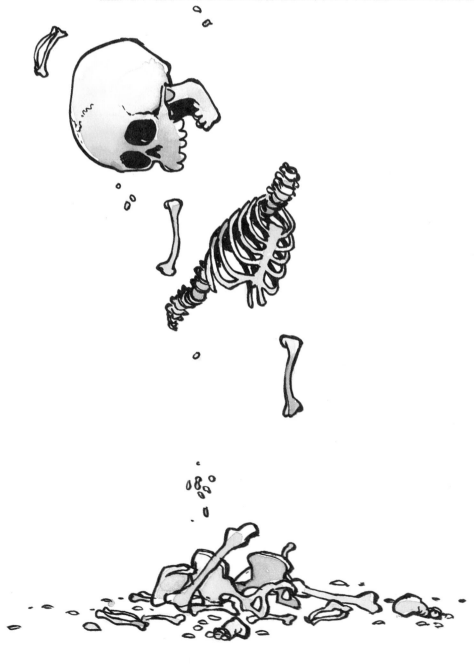

I know this 'cause I read it not
Two hours ago, and then I got
The heebie-jeebies and these awful shakes.

My parents swore upon their honor
That I was safe, and not a goner.
I guess tomorrow they'll see their sad mistakes.

Dad will look at Mom and say,
"Too bad he had to go that way."
And Mom will look at Dad, and nod assent.

Mom will add, "Still, it's fitting,
That as he was this world quitting,
He should leave another mess before he went."

They may not mind at first, I know.
They will miss me later, though,
And perhaps admit that they were wrong.
As memories of me grow dim,
They'll say, "We were too strict with him.
We should have listened to him all along."

Here Lies
CALVIN
DEVOURED IN HIS
BED BY A MONSTER

If Only We Had
Treated Him Better

As speedily my end approaches,
I bid a final "buenas noches"
To my best friend here in all the world.
Gently snoring, whiskers seeming
To sniff at smells (he must be dreaming),
He lies snuggled in the blankets, curled.

HEY! WAKE UP, YOU STUPID CRETIN!
YOU GONNA SLEEP WHILE I GET EATEN?!
Suddenly the monster knows I'm not alone!

There's an animal in bed with me!
An awful beast he did not see!
The monster never would've come if he had known!

SO LONG, POP! I'M OFF TO CHECK MY TIGER TRAP!

I RIGGED A TUNA FISH SANDWICH YESTERDAY, SO I'M **SURE** TO HAVE A TIGER BY NOW!

THEY LIKE TUNA FISH, HUH?

TIGERS WILL DO **ANYTHING** FOR A TUNA FISH SANDWICH!

WE'RE KIND OF STUPID THAT WAY.

MUNCH MUNCH

SO DAD, WHAT DO I DO WHEN I CATCH A TIGER?

BRING IT HOME AND STUFF IT, CALVIN! CAN'T YOU SEE I'M BUSY?

SHEESH.

NO, REALLY, I COULDN'T EAT ANOTHER BITE!

WHAT'S ALL THIS NOISE? YOU'RE SUPPOSED TO BE ASLEEP!

IT WAS HOBBES, DAD! HE WAS JUMPING ON THE BED! HONEST!

"HOBBES" WAS **NOT** JUMPING ON THE BED! NOW GO TO SLEEP!

YOU WERE **TOO** JUMPING ON THE BED!

WELL, **YOU** WERE THE ONE PLAYING THE CYMBALS!!

SHOW AND TELL IS OVER, CALVIN. PLEASE PUT YOUR "TIGER" IN YOUR LOCKER.

IN MY LOCKER?! HE'LL SUFFOCATE!

WELL, AT LEAST PUT HIM UNDER YOUR CHAIR.

WHEW! THAT WAS A CLOSE ONE!

I'LL SAY!

SEVEN PLUS THREE.

SEVENTY-THREE.

WATTERSON

GOOD NIGHT, CALVIN.

'NIGHT, DAD!

HEY! AREN'T YOU GOING TO SAY GOOD NIGHT TO HOBBES?!

GOOD NIGHT, HOBBES.

THAT'S IT?! NO STORY? NO SMOOCH??

GO TO SLEEP, YOU SISSY.

WATTERSON

WHAT'S THIS?

TASTE IT. YOU'LL LOVE IT.

YOU KNOW YOU'LL HATE SOMETHING WHEN THEY WON'T TELL YOU WHAT IT IS.

WATTERSON

CalviN aNd HobbES by WATTERSON

OUTRAGE! WHY SHOULD I GO TO BED? I'M NOT TIRED! IT'S ONLY 7:30! THIS IS TYRANNY! I'M!

GOOD NIGHT, CALVIN.

WILL YOU CHECK FOR MONSTERS UNDER THE BED?

NO MONSTERS. YOU'RE SAFE.

WHAT ABOUT IN THE DRESSER?

WATTERSON

CALVIN, I'M SURE THERE ARE NO MONSTERS IN YOUR DRESSER. GO TO SLEEP.

GREAT. I'LL BET THAT'S WHERE THEY ALL ARE. THEY'LL COME OUT AND KILL US AS SOON AS WE FALL ASLEEP.

SO WHO'S GOING TO FALL ASLEEP?

WELL, WE'LL JUST HAVE TO GET THE MONSTERS FIRST. YOU IRRITATE THEM WITH THIS HORN, AND I'LL NAIL 'EM WITH MY DART GUN WHEN THEY COME OUT!

GET READY! I HEAR ONE COMING!

HONK HONK HONK HONK HONK HON HONK

WHAT'S ALL THE NOISE?!

AAIEEE!! A MONSTER IN THE HALLWAY!!

DEAR, WILL YOU COME UP HERE A MINUTE?

I THINK I WOUNDED HIM. GIVE ME THE BAT AND I'LL FINISH HIM OFF!

21

caLviN and HobbES by WATERSON

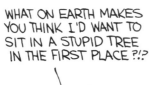

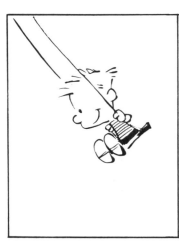

Calvin and Hobbes by WATTERSON

OUR HERO, THE VALIANT SPACEMAN SPIFF, IS MAROONED ON A STRANGE WORLD...

I'LL SET MY MERTILIZER ON "DEEP FAT FRY."

CALVIN! YOU'RE NOT PAYING ATTENTION!

...WE JOIN SPACEMAN SPIFF ON THE DISTANT PLANET ZORG...

GRONK! ARGH!

ZOUNDS!

TRAPPED BY A HIDEOUS GRAKNIL, SPIFF DRAWS HIS TRUSTY ATOMIC NAPALM NEUTRALIZER!

CHEW ELECTRIC DEATH, SNARLING CUR!

BUT THE WEAPON IS USELESS! SPIFF IS DOOMED!!

OUR HERO MAKES A BREAK, AND DUCKS INTO A NEARBY CAVE!

WEEOOO! WHAT'S THAT AWFUL SMELL?

EEP!

TEACHERS LOUNGE

WHO WAS *THAT*?

BEATS ME, FRED.

SLAM!

WATTERSON

WE JOIN OUR HERO MEGAZORKS ABOVE PLANET GLOOB...

SPACEMAN SPIFF, CONQUEROR OF THE COSMOS, IS PURSUED BY THE HIDEOUS SCUM BEINGS OF PLANET Q-13!

SPIFF'S HYPER-FREEM DRIVE MALFUNCTIONS! THE ALIENS CLOSE IN!

SUDDENLY, A SEARING BOLT OF DEADLY FRAP RAY SLICES ACROSS THE BLACKNESS! OUR HERO IS UNFAZED.

ANOTHER BOLT! SPIFF IS HIT!!

PLOOIE!

SPIFF IS GOING DOWN! CAN HE MAKE IT?? IS THIS THE END?!?

AAAAAA

SPIFF'S ALIVE! HE MADE IT!!

I'M ALIVE! HA HA HA! I KISS THE SWEET GROUND!

MAYBE YOU SHOULD PLAY ON THE SWINGS, CALVIN.

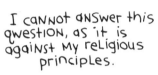

44

HI, DAD. IT'S ME, CALVIN!

HOW'S WORK GOING? ...UH HUH... PRETTY DAY OUT, ISN'T IT? ... YEP.....

ARE YOU BRINGING ME HOME ANY PRESENTS TONIGHT? ... NO? WELL, JUST THOUGHT I'D ASK...

LISTEN, I SUPPOSE YOU'RE WONDERING WHY I CALLED...

DAD, YOUR POLLS TOOK A BIG DIVE THIS WEEK.

YOUR "OVERALL DAD PERFORMANCE" RATING WAS ESPECIALLY LOW.

SEE? RIGHT ABOUT YESTERDAY YOUR POPULARITY WENT DOWN THE TUBES.

CALVIN, YOU DIDN'T GET DESSERT YESTERDAY BECAUSE YOU FLOODED THE HOUSE!!

I'D SUGGEST A NEW LINE OF WORK, "DAD"...

THE GIANT SLIMY OCTOPUS OOZES ACROSS THE BEACH.

HIS HIDEOUS PRESENCE TERRORIZES THE SLEEPY WATERFRONT COMMUNITY.

WITH A SUCKER-COVERED TENTACLE, HE GRABS AN UNSUSPECTING TOURIST.

A MUFFLED SCREAM LINGERS IN THE SALTY AIR!

DID YOU WANT SOMETHING, CALVIN?

ACK ICK IG

53

WAKE UP, CALVIN. IT'S TIME FOR SCHOOL.

I'M NOT GOING TO SCHOOL ANYMORE.

YOU HAVE TO. IT'S THE LAW.

WATTERSON

WHAT ABOUT HOBBES? WHY DOESN'T *HE* HAVE TO GO TO SCHOOL?

HE'S A TIGER. GET UP.

WHAT'S BEING A TIGER GOT TO DO WITH IT?

TIGERS WRECK THE GRADE CURVE.

DO YOU THINK IT'S BETTER TO LIVE IN STUPEFYING SECURITY...

...OR TO TAKE RISKS AND LIVE LIFE ON THE EDGE?

I THINK IT'S BETTER TO ACCEPT DANGER AND LIVE TO THE FULLEST!

I TAKE IT BY YOUR SILENCE THAT YOU AGREE...

WATTERSON

I'M MAKING SUSIE DERKINS A VALENTINE.

SHE'S A CUTIE, ALL RIGHT.

SEE, I MADE A BIG RED HEART.

WATTERSON

NOW I'M PUTTING LACE AROUND IT.

THAT'S VERY SWEET. I'M SURE SHE'LL LIKE IT.

Susie,
I hate you. Drop dead.
Calvin

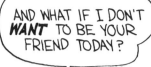

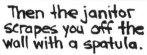

CALVIN, YOU'RE NOT PAYING ATTENTION AGAIN!

SPACEMAN SPIFF, CONQUEROR OF THE COSMOS, IS TRAPPED BY A HIDEOUS ZONDARG!

WITH LIGHTNING SPEED, SPIFF BOLTS FOR THE AIR LOCK, MAKING A DARING ESCAPE!

NICE TRY, CALVIN.

I'M HOME!

DID YOU FEED HOBBES TODAY, MOM?

NO, DEAR, IT MUST HAVE SLIPPED MY MIND.

THANKS, MOM. YOU WANNA JUST DOUSE ME IN STEAK SAUCE BEFORE I GO TO MY ROOM?

MOMMMM!

I'M THIRSTY!

WHAT'S THIS? JUST WATER?

CaLviN and HObbeS
by WATTERSON

HEY MOM, CAN **I** DRIVE NOW?

NO.

HOW ABOUT **NOW**?

KLUNK

OH NO!

OH YOU STUPID CAR! WHAT'S WRONG WITH YOU **NOW**?!?

THAT'S IT, MOM! GO AHEAD AND SWEAR! WE DON'T MIND!

CALVIN, BE QUIET!

WANT HOBBES AND ME TO GO GET HELP?

YOU STAY WHERE YOU ARE. I'LL LOOK UNDER THE HOOD.

KICK THE CAR, MOM! IT WORKS ON THE TV!

LOOK AT ALL THESE CARS GOING BY. NOBODY'S STOPPING TO HELP.

LET'S BLOW THE HORN! MAYBE SOMEONE WILL COME.

BEEEEP!
AAUGH!
BEEP! BEEP!

HOORAYY!!
SOMEONE STOPPED! WE'RE HEROES!!

WANT ME TO CALL A TOW TRUCK, LADY?

FIRST CALL THE POLICE AND REPORT AN INFANTICIDE.

I NEED HELP ON MY HOMEWORK. WHAT'S A PRONOUN?

A NOUN THAT LOST ITS AMATEUR STATUS.

MAYBE I CAN GET A POINT FOR ORIGINALITY.

LEAVE YOUR TIGER IN THE CAR, CALVIN.

CAN'T HOBBES COME ALONG, DAD? HE WON'T EAT ANYBODY!

NO, CALVIN. LET'S GO.

WELL, AT LEAST LET ME OPEN THE WINDOW AND GIVE HIM SOME AIR.

SEE IF HE'LL LEAVE THE KEYS, TOO, SO I CAN LISTEN TO THE RADIO.

CALVIN, YOUR MOTHER AND I HAVE DECIDED TO GIVE YOU AN ALLOWANCE.

IT'S IMPORTANT THAT ONE LEARNS THE VALUE OF MONEY.

MONEY! HA HA HA! I'M RICH! I'M RICH! I CAN BUY OFF ANYONE! THE WORLD IS MINE!

POWER! FRIENDS! PRESTIGE!

I BLEW IT AGAIN, DEAR!

I CAN BUY IT ALL! I'M FREE! HA HA HA HA!

You're gonna taste asphalt fifth period, Twinky. Just so you know.

GREAT. I'M DEAD.

FIFTH PERIOD - "STUDIES IN CONTEMPORARY STATE-SPONSORED TERRORISM."

...ALSO KNOWN AS GYM CLASS.

WATTERSON

I CAN'T GET A BABY SITTER ANYWHERE! WHAT SHOULD WE DO?

WE WON'T BE GONE LONG. COULDN'T CALVIN BE LEFT FOR A COUPLE HOURS UNSUPERVISED?

WATTERSON

HA HA HA HA HA!
HO HO HO HO HEE HE
HA
HOO HO
HO

...SERIOUSLY... WHAT SHOULD WE DO?

HEE HEE

OKAY, CALVIN, WE'LL BE BACK IN A COUPLE OF HOURS.

YOU AND HOBBES JUST WATCH TV AND BE GOOD, OKAY?

WATTERSON

DID YOU HEAR THAT? WE GET TO WATCH TV!!

HOORAY!

VIDEORAMA? I'D LIKE TO RENT A VCR AND SOME MOVIES!

ASK IF THEY HAVE "ATTACK OF THE COED CANNIBALS."

64

WELL, THE HOUSE IS STILL STANDING. CALVIN MUST HAVE GONE TO BED.

HIS LIGHT IS STILL ON. ...CALVIN? ARE YOU AWAKE?

EEP!

DID YOU WATCH A SCARY MOVIE?!?

NO. DON'T COME IN. THE RUG IS RIGGED TOO.

WHAP!

SMASH

TINKLE
DING
SHATTER
CLINK

WOW. FIRST TRY!

DOWNTOWN TOKYO!

AARRGHHGH!

GODZILLA.

Calvin and Hobbes
by WATTERSON

HOW CAN I GET SOME MONEY?

...SHORT OF EARNING IT, I MEAN...

I WANT A GRENADE LAUNCHER, MOM. WHEN'S CHRISTMAS?

NOT FOR A LONG TIME.

WHEN'S MY BIRTHDAY?

NOT FOR A LONG TIME.

WHEN'S MY ALLOWANCE?

YOU SPENT IT ALREADY.

DO I HAVE ANY STOCKS I CAN CASH? WAR BONDS??

CALVIN, I'M TRYING TO WORK!

CAN I BORROW SOME SOAP?

YES, YOU CAN BORROW SOME SOAP. HAVE ALL THE SOAP YOU WANT.

4 SALE CHEEP!

HOW ARE YOU TODAY?

FINE.

I WANT THE TOP OF MY HEAD SHAVED, AND THE SIDES DYED PINK AND CUT IN HORIZONTAL STRIPES, OK?

MA'AM?

GIVE HIM THE USUAL, PETE.

WELL I GUESS THIS GUY KNOWS WHICH SIDE *HIS* BREAD IS BUTTERED ON!

THERE, HOW'S THAT LOOK?

THAT'S GREAT. PERFECT.

WITHOUT QUESTION, THIS IS THE FINEST HAIRCUT I HAVE EVER RECEIVED.

NEVER CRITICIZE A GUY WITH A RAZOR...

TOO BAD THE WORLD WILL BE ENDING SOON.

BEG YOUR PARDON?

HALLEY'S COMET. COMETS ARE HARBINGERS OF DOOM.

NO, THEY AREN'T. THAT'S JUST SUPERSTITION.

REALLY??

GUESS I'D BETTER WRITE THAT BOOK REPORT.

TOLL BOOTH, DAD! YOU CAN'T PUT THE CAR IN UNTIL YOU PAY ME A QUARTER!

WHY SHOULD I PAY YOU TO PUT *MY* CAR IN *MY* GARAGE?

BECAUSE IF YOU DON'T, I'LL PULL THE DOOR DOWN ON THE HOOD AS YOU DRIVE IN!

WHAT A CHEAPSKATE.

A LITTLE LOWER...OK, FINE!

THANKS FOR HELPING ME PUT UP THIS SWING.

WHERE DID YOU EVER FIND THIS GREAT TIRE?

CALVIN! I'VE GOT TO GO TO WORK!!

WHAT'S THAT CEREAL YOU'RE EATING?

IT'S MY NEW FAVORITE, "CHOCOLATE FROSTED SUGAR BOMBS."

HAVE A TASTE.

THANK YOU.

MFFPBTH!! S-SW-SW SNEET!!

ACTUALLY, THEY'RE KINDA BLAND TILL YOU SCOOP SUGAR ON 'EM.

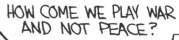

RISE AND SHINE, CALVIN!

MFGPBTHBBPT

THE EARLY BIRD GETS THE WORM!

BIG INCENTIVE.

I'VE DECIDED WE SHOULD BE "COOLER" THAN WE ARE.

WE'RE NOT COOL?

SURE WE'RE COOL. BUT WE'RE NOT AS COOL AS WE *COULD* BE.

COOL PEOPLE WEAR DARK GLASSES!

IT'S COOL TO BUMP INTO THINGS?

YOU DON'T MOVE, YOU JUST HANG AROUND.

HEY, DAD, WILL YOU BUY ME A FLAME THROWER?

OF COURSE NOT. DON'T BE SILLY.

EVEN IF I DIDN'T USE IT IN THE HOUSE?

SOMEWHERE IN COMMUNIST RUSSIA I'LL BET THERE'S A LITTLE BOY WHO HAS NEVER KNOWN ANYTHING BUT **CENSORSHIP** AND **OPPRESSION**.

BUT MAYBE HE'S HEARD ABOUT **AMERICA**, AND HE DREAMS OF LIVING IN THIS LAND OF **FREEDOM** AND OPPORTUNITY!

SOMEDAY, I'D LIKE TO MEET THAT LITTLE BOY...

...AND TELL HIM THE AWFUL **TRUTH** ABOUT THIS PLACE!!

CALVIN, BE QUIET AND EAT THE STUPID LIMA BEANS.

WHENEVER I TAKE MY BATH...

...I ALWAYS PUT MY DUCKY IN FIRST.

FOR COMPANIONSHIP?

TO TEST FOR SHARKS.

MY SECRET ANCIENT TREASURE MAP SAYS TO DIG HERE!

LOOK! A WALLET FULL OF MONEY! RIGHT WHERE YOU SAID!

IT'S DAD'S. I BURIED IT HERE LAST WEEK.

SPACEMAN SPIFF, BOLD INTERPLANETARY EXPLORER, SPIES A ZARG!

SPIFF CALIBRATES HIS BLASTER. READY...AIM...

CALVIN, IF YOU SHOOT THAT PAPER CLIP AT ME, I'LL GET YOUR BOTTOM HAULED TO THE PRINCIPAL'S OFFICE SO FAST YOU'LL THINK YOU WERE IN A **TIME WARP!!**

CONFOUND IT. THE BLASTER JAMMED.

IT LOOKS LIKE HOBBES BURST A SEAM HERE. I'LL GET MY SEWING KIT.

IT'S JUST A LITTLE CUT. I DON'T NEED AN OPERATION. THIS IS UNNECESSARY SURGERY!

IT'S NOT SURGERY. YOU'RE JUST GETTING A COUPLE STITCHES! WHAT'S THE BIG DEAL?

YOUR MOM NEVER USES ANY ANESTHETIC.

WHAT A PECULIAR DREAM I HAD LAST NIGHT!

I DREAMED I WAS IN A BIG FIGHT WITH A FEROCIOUS WEASEL!

WHAT DO YOU SUPPOSE IT MEANS?

IT MEANS YOU'RE SLEEPING ON THE FLOOR TONIGHT, YOU NINCOMPOOP!

WHERE'S MY JACKET?

I'VE LOOKED EVERYWHERE! UNDER THE BED, OVER MY CHAIR...

...ON THE STAIRS, ON THE HALL FLOOR, IN THE KITCHEN... IT'S JUST NOT ANYWHERE!

OH, *HERE* IT IS! WHO PUT IT IN THE STUPID CLOSET?!?

HOCUS-POCUS, ABRACADABRA!

I COMMAND MY HOMEWORK TO DO ITSELF! **HOMEWORK, BE DONE!**

FLIP FLIP FLIP

RATS.

DO YOU EVER THINK ABOUT THE END OF THE WORLD AS WE KNOW IT?

YOU MEAN A NUCLEAR WAR?

I THINK MOM WAS REFERRING TO IF SHE EVER CATCHES ME LETTING THE AIR OUT OF THE CAR TIRES AGAIN.

FEARLESS SPACEMAN SPIFF CLOSES IN ON THE FLEEING ZARGONS!

ONCE AGAIN OUR HERO IS ABOUT TO TEACH VICIOUS ALIEN SCUM THAT VIRTUE IS ITS OWN REWARD! HE LOCKS ONTO TARGET!

PSST, CALVIN! WHAT WAS THE CAPITAL OF POLAND UNTIL 1600?

KRAKOW.

THANKS.

KRAKOW! KRAKOW! TWO DIRECT HITS!

WATTERSON

THE TYRANNOSAURUS LUMBERS ACROSS THE PREHISTORIC VALLEY...

THE TERRIFYING LIZARD IS THREE STORIES TALL AND HIS MOUTH IS FILLED WITH SIX-INCH CHISELS OF DEATH!

WITH A FEW MIGHTY STEPS, THE DINOSAUR IS UPON A TRIBE OF FLEEING CAVEMEN. HE DEVOURS THEM ONE BY ONE!

AARRGH! AAIEEE! AAUGHH!

CALVIN, EAT YOUR POPCORN QUIETLY!

WATTERSON

WHAT DOES THIS WORD MEAN?

WHICH ONE?

THAT LONG ONE.

!

WATTERSON

I DON'T KNOW.

YOU DO TOO!! ALL RIGHT! WHERE'S A DICTIONARY??

WHACK!

WOW! ANOTHER HOLE IN ONE!

WOW! THREE NEW MAGAZINES FOR ME TODAY.

YESTERDAY I GOT FIVE. I LOVE GETTING ALL THIS MAIL.

HOW COME YOU RECEIVE ALL THESE MAGAZINES?

I WENT TO THE LIBRARY AND FILLED OUT ALL THE SUBSCRIPTION CARDS THAT SAID "BILL ME LATER".

I LOVE SATURDAY MORNING CARTOONS.

WHAT CLASSIC HUMOR!

THIS IS WHAT ENTERTAINMENT IS ALL ABOUT.

... IDIOTS, EXPLOSIVES, AND FALLING ANVILS.

CALVIN, THE HUMAN INSECT, WALKS ACROSS THE DINNER TABLE.

WITH PROPORTIONAL INSECT STRENGTH, HE PLACES A GIANT PEA ON THE EDGE OF A SPOON.

HE THEN CLIMBS TO THE TOP OF THE OTHER END...

...AND WITH A TINY JUMP...

CALVIN, STOP THAT!

IN HIS MINUSCULE SIZE, IT TAKES CALVIN, THE HUMAN INSECT, TEN MINUTES TO WALK ACROSS A BOOK'S PAGE!

AT THE OTHER END, HE SLOWLY LIFTS THE GIGANTIC SHEET!

THEN IT'S ANOTHER TEN-MINUTE JOURNEY BACK, AS HE TURNS IT OVER!

GEE, THE KID'S BEEN QUIET FOR ALMOST TWENTY MINUTES.

HE'S DOING HIS HOMEWORK.

HERE'S A MOVIE WE SHOULD WATCH.

WHO'S IN IT?

IT SAYS, "JAPANESE CAST."

"TWO BIG RUBBERY MONSTERS SLUG IT OUT OVER MAJOR METROPOLITAN CENTERS IN A BATTLE FOR WORLD SUPREMACY."

DOESN'T THAT SOUND GREAT?

AND PEOPLE SAY THAT FOREIGN FILM IS INACCESSIBLE.

OH, ROSALYN, YOU'RE HERE! GOOD, COME IN!

WE REALLY APPRECIATE YOUR COMING ON SUCH SHORT NOTICE. WE'VE HAD A TERRIBLE TIME GETTING A BABY SITTER FOR TONIGHT.

HA HA, MAYBE LITTLE CALVIN HERE HAS GOTTEN HIMSELF A REPUTATION.

HA HA. YOU HAVE THE HALF UP FRONT?

YES, LET ME GET MY PURSE...

HI, BABY DOLL, IT'S ME. YEAH, I'M BABY SITTING THE KID DOWN THE STREET.

YEAH, THAT'S RIGHT, THE LITTLE MONSTER. ...HMM?... WELL SO FAR, NO PROBLEM.

HE HASN'T BEEN ANY TROUBLE. YOU JUST HAVE TO SHOW THESE KIDS WHO'S THE BOSS. ...MM HMM..

HOW MUCH LONGER TILL SHE LETS US OUT OF THE GARAGE?

SHE SAID 8 O'CLOCK, AND IT'S ALMOST 6:30 NOW...

THANKS AGAIN FOR BABY SITTING, ROSALYN.

CALVIN WAS NO TROUBLE AT ALL.

THAT'S GOOD. I'LL GET THE CAR AND DRIVE YOU HOME.

THERE YOU GO. GOOD NIGHT.

THANK YOU. GOOD NIGHT.

IS SHE GONE?

96

97

GRAB THE HOTDOGS AND COME ON!

THE TROOP'S COOKING DINNER OVER THE FIRE.

OH THAT'S JUST GREAT.

HERE WE'VE BEEN LUGGING THIS DUMB MICROWAVE AROUND FOR NOTHING.

BOP

SPIKE!

OH OH, WE'D BETTER LEAVE!

IT LOOKS LIKE SOME BIG PEOPLE WANT TO PLAY TENNIS.

THE CROCODILE FLOATS TO THE TOP OF THE MURKY AMAZON...

COMPLETELY MOTIONLESS, HE APPEARS TO BE ONLY A HARMLESS LOG.

A HIPPOPOTAMUS APPROACHES AND ENSURES ITS INSTANT DEATH!

CALVIN, WHAT ARE YOU DOING? ARE YOU ALL RIGHT?

CLOSER... CLOSER...

WELL LOOK, SOMEBODY LEFT A STUFFED TIGER OUT IN THE FIELD. HOW STRANGE.

LOOKS LIKE A DOG'S BEEN CHEWING ON YOU, FELLA.

WELL, NOTHING A LITTLE TEA PARTY WITH SOME OTHER STUFFED ANIMALS WOULDN'T HELP. C'MON.

HOBBES! HOBBES! WHERE ARE YOU ??

HELLO, CALVIN. WOULD YOU LIKE TO JOIN MY TEA PARTY?

HECK NO. I'M TRYING TO FIND MY BEST FRIEND, WHO'S BEEN KIDNAPPED BY A DOG. LEAVE ME ALONE.

WELL I THINK MR. CALVIN IS VERY RUDE, DON'T YOU, MR. TIGER? YES, I THINK SO TOO. MORE TEA, ANYONE?

HEY, I SHOULD TELL SUSIE TO KEEP HER EYES OPEN FOR HOBBES.

SUSIE, I... HOBBES!

YOU FOUND HOBBES! THANK YOU THANK YOU THANKYOUTHANKYOUTHANKY OUTHANKYOUTHANKYOUTHA

WELL! WASN'T MR. CALVIN A GENTLEMAN! I DO HOPE... HEY! WHO TOOK ALL THE COOKIES ?!?

SUSIE, WANNA HEAR A SECRET?

SURE.

I THINK THE PRINCIPAL IS A SPACE ALIEN SPY.

HE'S TRYING TO CORRUPT OUR YOUNG INNOCENT MINDS SO WE'LL BE UNABLE TO RESIST WHEN HIS PEOPLE INVADE EARTH!

PROMISE NOT TO TELL ANYONE?

DON'T WORRY.

HOBBES, WHAT SHOULD I DO WHEN MOE COMES TO BEAT ME UP IN GYM CLASS?

WELL, YOU CAN ALWAYS DO WHAT WE TIGERS DO WHEN A RHINO CHARGES.

WHAT'S THAT?

WE SCRAMBLE LIKE MANIACS FOR THE NEAREST TREE.

THAT'S YOUR ADVICE?? TO SIT IN A TREE ALL DAY?!?

IT DOESN'T IMPRESS THE GIRLS, OF COURSE, BUT THERE'S NO SENSE IMPRESSING THEM AND THEN GETTING KILLED, MY DAD USED TO SAY...

HOBBES, I NEED YOUR HELP. THAT BULLY MOE KEEPS PUSHING ME AROUND.

...SO I WANT YOU TO COME TO SCHOOL AND EAT HIM, OK?

EAT HIM?

SURE! TIGERS EAT PEOPLE ALL THE TIME!

WHAT IF THE CAFETERIA LADIES WON'T LET ME USE THE OVEN?

IT'S TOO EARLY TO BE IN BED. IT'S HARDLY EVEN DARK OUT. WHY DO I HAVE TO BE IN BED? IT'S RIDICULOUS.

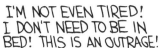

I'M NOT EVEN TIRED! I DON'T NEED TO BE IN BED! THIS IS AN OUTRAGE!

IT'S THE STUPIDEST THING I CAN IMAGINE! I THINK MOM AND DAD ARE JUST TRYING TO GET RID OF ME. I CAN'T SLEEP AT ALL. CAN YOU SLEEP, HOBBES?

NO!

WATTERSON

OK, MOM, HOBBES AND I HAVE FORMED A LOBBY. WE WANT MORE PRIVILEGES!

MORE PRIVILEGES? LIKE WHAT? YOU'VE GOT IT MADE!

WATTERSON

NO RESPONSIBILITIES, NO CARES, NO WORRIES! WHAT MORE COULD YOU POSSIBLY WANT?

WHY DIDN'T YOU TELL HER ABOUT THE CREDIT CARDS IN OUR NAMES?

YOU HEARD HER. SHE'S IN ONE OF HER MOODS.

I LOVE SATURDAYS!

EVERY SATURDAY I GET UP AT SIX AND EAT THREE BOWLS OF CRUNCHY SUGAR BOMBS.

THEN I WATCH CARTOONS TILL NOON, AND I'M INCOHERENT AND HYPERACTIVE THE REST OF THE DAY.

WATTERSON

DOES IT WORK?

NO BROTHERS OR SISTERS SO FAR!

EVERYBODY I KNOW HAS EITHER CABLE TV OR A VCR! THEY CAN WATCH ANYTHING THEY WANT!

BUT ME? *I* HAVE TO WATCH DUMB OL' SUMMER REPEATS! *I* HAVE TO WATCH THE SAME GARBAGE OVER AND OVER!

HOW CRUELLY WE MISTREAT YOU, CALVIN.

...SO THEN HE GAVE ME "OLIVER TWIST" TO READ, AND SAID I MIGHT IDENTIFY WITH IT.

RATS...AND "SORORITY ROW HORROR" IS ON CABLE TONIGHT.

I GOT A HELIUM BALLOON.

VERY NICE.

I'M GOING TO STAND ON THIS LADDER AND LET THE BALLOON CARRY ME UP AND AWAY.

NOTHING'S HAPPENING.

TRY JUMPING.

SEE? THERE GOES THE BALLOON. YOU DIDN'T HANG ON.

FLUSH!

WHEEE! HA HA HA!

I'M DONE WITH MY BATH.

MM... THAT WAS QUICK.

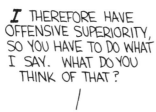

WHEN ARE WE GOING TO GET TO OUR VACATION SITE? I WANNA *BE* THERE!

CALVIN, IT'S AN EIGHT-HOUR DRIVE. WE'RE NOT EVEN OUT OF OUR STATE YET. IT'S GOING TO BE A WHILE. RELAX.

HOW MUCH LONGER *NOW*?

I TOLD YOU WE SHOULD HAVE FLOWN.

THERE'S A RESTAURANT COMING UP. WANT TO STOP?

ONLY IF THEY HAVE HAMBURGERS.

HAMBURGERS? THAT'S ALL WE'VE EATEN THIS WHOLE STUPID TRIP! HAMBURGERS, HAMBURGERS, HAMBURGERS!

I'M SICK OF HAMBURGERS! WE'RE EATING SOMETHING ELSE FOR ONCE!

TEN MILLION BOTTLES OF BEER ON THE WALL, TEN MILLION BOTTLES OF BEER...

OK! OK! HERE'S A HAMBURGER JOINT! *ARE YOU HAPPY?!*

I HAVE TO GO TO THE BATHROOM.

CALVIN, WE JUST PULLED OUT OF THE RESTAURANT. CAN'T YOU WAIT? THINK OF SOMETHING ELSE.

ALL I CAN THINK OF IS NIAGARA FALLS, AND THE HOOVER DAM, AND NOAH'S ARK, AND...

OOH BOY, NOW *I* HAVE TO GO!

NEXT YEAR I SWEAR I'LL JUST TAKE A VACATION BY MYSELF.

Calvin and Hobbes by WATTERSON

IT'S ANOTHER NEW MORNING FOR MR. MONROE. HE GLANCES AT THE NEWSPAPER HEADLINES OVER A CUP OF COFFEE, AND GETS IN HIS RED SPORTS CAR TO GO TO WORK.

LITTLE DOES HE REALIZE IT'S HIS LAST DAY ON THE FACE OF THE EARTH!

CALVIN DRINKS THE MAGIC ELIXIR AND BEGINS AN INCREDIBLE TRANSFORMATION!

INSTANTLY HE GROWS! BIGGER AND BIGGER! HIGHER AND HIGHER!

HE IS NOW OVER 300 FEET TALL! THE FORMULA IS A SUCCESS!

CALVIN, THE MIGHTY GIANT, GOES ON A TERRIBLE RAMPAGE, STRIKING FEAR INTO THE HEARTS OF THE POPULACE!

NOTHING CAN STOP HIM! IT'S PANIC IN THE STREETS! A TOWN LIES IN RUINS!

NO, I WON'T BUY YOU ANY MORE TOY CARS. *I* SAW YOU! YOU DELIBERATELY STOMPED ON THOSE!

C'MON, CALVIN! I SIGNED YOU UP FOR SWIMMING LESSONS.

I DON'T *WANT* SWIMMING LESSONS.!!

TOO LATE. LET'S GO.

WHAT ABOUT HOBBES? DID YOU SIGN HIM UP TOO?

NO, IT'S NOT GOOD TO GET TIGERS WET.

WHY IS *THAT*?

IT TAKES US ALL DAY TO DRY, AND UNTIL WE DO, WE SMELL FUNNY.

I CAN'T BELIEVE MY MOM SIGNED ME UP FOR SWIMMING LESSONS.

HERE I AM FREEZING MY BUNS OFF AT 9 IN THE MORNING, ABOUT TO JUMP INTO ICE WATER AND DROWN.

THE ONLY THING THAT COULD POSSIBLY MAKE THIS WORSE WOULD BE IF THE CLASS WAS...

...TAUGHT BY MY SADISTIC BABY SITTER!!

WELL, LOOK WHO'S HERE!

OK.... EVERYONE IN THE WATER!

I REFUSE! I'M FREEZING ALREADY!

CALVIN, DO YOU KNOW WHAT A "RAT TAIL" IS?

NO.

IT'S WHEN YOU SOAK A TOWEL AND TWIST IT UP INTO A WHIP. IT STINGS LIKE CRAZY AND IS MUCH WORSE THAN BEING COLD. GET MY DRIFT?

I ALWAYS THOUGHT LIFE-GUARDS WERE JUST TAUGHT HOW TO RESUSCITATE PEOPLE AND THINGS LIKE THAT.

THIS WATER IS FREEZING! I'M GOING TO GO INTO SHOCK AND DROWN, I JUST KNOW IT.

I BET THE LIFEGUARD IS INVOLVED IN SOME INSURANCE SCAM AND SHE'S GOING TO LET US ALL DROWN LIKE RATS! OH NO! OH NO!

OK, FIRST WE'RE GOING TO LEARN THE "DEADMAN'S FLOAT."

MOM!! HELPP! HELPP!

WHAT I PUT UP WITH TO PAY FOR COLLEGE..

I DON'T WANT TO LEARN HOW TO SWIM!

I DON'T NEED TO KNOW HOW. I'LL JUST STAY ON DRY LAND ALL MY LIFE.

WHAT IF YOU FALL OUT OF A BOAT?

NO BIG DEAL.

FORTY MINUTES OF TERROR! WHY DID YOU SIGN ME UP FOR THIS?

WHY NOT SOMETHING FUN, LIKE HANG GLIDING OR SHARPSHOOTING?

...OR *DRIVING* LESSONS! I COULD BE TAKING DRIVING LESSONS AND LEARNING SOMETHING USEFUL!

HOW ABOUT PIANO LESSONS? YOU START TUESDAY.

ACK! NO NO NO NO NO NO NO NO NO

HEY, MOM, ARE YOU NERVOUS?

NO. ...WHY?

CALVIN, GO OUTSIDE AND QUIT BUGGING ME!

CALVIN THE BUG BUZZES OFF!

FLYING LOW OVER THE GRASS, HE SEARCHES FOR DEAD MEAT!

UP AND OVER THE FLOWERS, DARTING THIS WAY AND THAT!

OH NO! HE'S CAUGHT IN A SPIDER WEB!

THRASHING ABOUT IN A DESPERATE BID FOR FREEDOM, HE ONLY BECOMES MORE ENTANGLED! SOON THE SPIDER WILL SUCK OUT HIS INNARDS! HELP!

I WAS GOING TO JOIN YOU IN THE HAMMOCK, BUT I THINK I'LL FORGET IT.

HI, CALVIN, WHAT ARE YOU DOING?

BIG IMPORTANT SECRET THINGS! GO AWAY! GET LOST!

ALL RIGHT, DANDELION HEAD! WHO CARES WHAT YOU DO ANYWAY!

WE'RE DOING GREAT THINGS. *WE'RE* HAVING FUN!

I THOUGHT WE WERE BORED OUT OF OUR SKULLS.

OH HUSH. YOU DON'T KNOW ANYTHING.

THAT STUPID CALVIN. HE'S SO MEAN.

ALL I TRY TO DO IS BE FRIENDS, AND HE TREATS ME LIKE I'M NOBODY.

WELL, WHO NEEDS JERKS LIKE HIM ANYWAY? I DON'T NEED HIM FOR A FRIEND. I CAN HAVE FUN BY MYSELF!

POOP.

SUSIE, HOBBES THOUGHT I WAS RUDE, SO I'M SORRY, AND YOU CAN COME PLAY WITH US IF YOU WANT.

THANKS, CALVIN. THAT'S REALLY NICE OF YOU.

OK, WE'LL PLAY HOUSE NOW. I'LL BE THE HIGH-POWERED EXECUTIVE WIFE, THE TIGER HERE CAN BE MY UNEMPLOYED, HOUSEKEEPING HUSBAND, AND YOU CAN BE OUR BRATTY AND BRAINLESS KID IN A DAY CARE CENTER.

THIS WAS *YOUR* IDEA, PEA BRAIN.

DON'T YOU TALK TO YOUR FATHER THAT WAY!

I'M OFF TO WALL STREET. DON'T WAIT UP.

LOOK AT THAT THING IN THE DIRT! IT MUST BE A FOSSIL!

I WONDER WHAT PECULIAR ANIMAL *THIS* WAS.

BUT IT'S NOT A BONE. IT MUST BE SOME PRIMITIVE HUNTING WEAPON OR EATING UTENSIL FOR CAVE MEN.

WATTERSON

MAYBE IT HAD SOME RELIGIOUS FUNCTION.

THIS EXPLAINS WHY YOUR CLOTHES STAY ON THE FLOOR.

MAKING A SIGN?

I'M DECLARING THE CREEK BACK IN THE WOODS "CALVIN'S CREEK."

WHEN YOU DISCOVER SOMETHING, YOU'RE ALLOWED TO NAME IT AND PUT UP A SIGN.

Calvin's CREEK

BUT SUPPOSE YOU DIDN'T DISCOVER THAT CREEK.

OF COURSE I DID! NOBODY *ELSE* HAS A SIGN THERE, RIGHT?

Hobs Crk

WATTERSON

CAN HOBBES AND I GO PLAY IN THE RAIN, MOM?

NO.

WHY NOT?

YOU'LL GET SOAKED.

WHAT'S WRONG WITH THAT?

YOU COULD CATCH PNEUMONIA, RUN UP A TERRIBLE HOSPITAL BILL, LINGER A FEW MONTHS, AND DIE.

I ALWAYS FORGET. IF YOU ASK A MOM, YOU GET A WORST-CASE SCENARIO.

I HAD NO IDEA THESE LITTLE SHOWERS WERE SO *DANGEROUS*.

WATTERSON

130

Calvin and Hobbes

by WATTERSON

YOU KNOW, DAD, IT DISTURBS ME THAT THIS WAGON HAS NO SEAT BELTS AND WOULDN'T SURVIVE A 30 MPH IMPACT WITH A STATIONARY OBJECT.

UM... WHY DO YOU BRING THIS UP?

OH, NO REASON.

WANT TO HELP ME TEST THE THEORY OF RELATIVITY?

SURE.

THE IDEA IS THAT THE FASTER WE GO, THE SLOWER TIME GOES.

GOTCHA. IT'S 10:23.

WHAT TIME IS IT NOW?

10:24. GO FASTER.

WE'RE GOING PRETTY FAST! WHAT TIME IS IT?

10:25. TIME STILL HASN'T STOPPED.

HAS TIME STOPPED *NOW*?

NO, JUST MY HEART.

WELL, IT LOOKS LIKE EINSTEIN'S A FRAUD, WOULDN'T YOU SAY?

NO, HE'S RIGHT! LOOK, MY WATCH ISN'T GOING AT ALL ANY MORE!!

"ADD TWO EGGS AND STIR."

RIGHT.

THE RECIPE SAYS IT MAKES TWENTY PANCAKES, SO WE'LL EACH GET TEN.

NAH, THAT'S TOO MUCH TROUBLE.

WE'LL JUST MAKE ONE *BIG* PANCAKE AND CUT IT IN HALF.

DAD, I WANT A BEDTIME STORY!

I'M BUSY, CALVIN. I'LL READ YOU ONE TOMORROW.

IF YOU DON'T READ ME A STORY, I WON'T GO TO BED!

①Once upon a time there was a boy named Calvin, who always wanted things his way. One day his dad got sick of it and locked him in the basement for the rest of his life. Everyone else lived happily ever after.
The End.

I DON'T LIKE THESE STORIES WITH MORALS.

DINNER'S READY, CALVIN. COME TO THE TABLE.

I'M WATCHING TELEVISION.

NO, YOU'RE NOT!

YES, I AM. I'M RIGHT HERE IN FRONT OF IT!

NO YOU'RE *NOT!*

OH THAT'S RIGHT. I'M AT THE TABLE.

Calvin and Hobbes by WATTERSON

WANNA TOSS THE OL' PIGSKIN AROUND?

HECK NO.

PHOOEY.

THE CENTER SNAPS THE BALL!

THE QUARTERBACK LOOKS FOR AN OPENING!

THE DEFENSE DISINTEGRATES BENEATH THE COMING ONSLAUGHT! THE QUARTERBACK JUMPS AND DODGES!

HOBBES BREAKS CLEAR!

CALVIN PASSES!

AN AMAZING CATCH! HOBBES IS AT THE 30...THE 20...THE 10...

...BUT HE'S TACKLED FROM BEHIND AND LATERALS TO CALVIN SO *HE* CAN MAKE THE TOUCHDOWN!

BUT CALVIN FUMBLES THE BALL AND HOBBES RECOVERS IT!

BUT A PENALTY IS CALLED ON THE PLAY AND HOBBES IS SENT TO THE BENCH!

HOBBES DEFECTS TO THE OTHER TEAM AND IS GREETED WITH ENTHUSIASTIC CHEERS! THE CROWD GOES WILD!

CALVIN PREPARES TO CRIPPLE THE TRAITOR WITH AN ILLEGAL FACE MASK PULL!

HOBBES DEFIES HIM BY POURING OUT HIS MOUTH GUARD ONTO CALVIN'S HELMET!

BOY, YOU CAN SEE WHY FOOTBALL IS SUCH A VIOLENT GAME!

HOBBES' TEAM GAINS A YARD! ALL THE CHEERLEADERS COME OUT FOR SMOOCHES!!

WATTERSON

138

I THINK I'M USING TOO STRONG A SUN SCREEN.

FISHING IS THE MOST BORING SPORT IN THE WORLD.

WE'VE BEEN SITTING HERE FOR TWENTY MINUTES AND NOT ONE THING HAS HAPPENED!

WAAUGHH!

YOU'RE ON MY HALF OF THE BED! MOVE OVER!

YOUR SIDE IS WAY OVER THERE! GIVE ME BACK THOSE COVERS!

CALVIN, BE QUIET AND GO TO SLEEP!!

YOU HEARD DAD. HE SAID TO GET ON YOUR SIDE AND LEAVE THE COVERS ALONE!

THAT'S NOT WHAT HE SAID! *HEY!* YOU STOLE MY PILLOW! THIS LUMPY ONE IS YOURS!

WITH A DRINK OF MAGIC ELIXIR, CALVIN TURNS HIMSELF INVISIBLE.

COMPLETELY TRANSPARENT, HE ROAMS UNDETECTED!

CALVIN?

BOY, AS SOON AS YOU WANT SOMETHING DONE AROUND HERE, THAT KID'S NOWHERE TO BE SEEN.

HA HA! I HAVE TURNED MYSELF INVISIBLE!

BY REMOVING MY CLOTHING, I CAN PERPETRATE ANY CRIME UNDETECTED!

I HAVE COMPLETE FREEDOM! I CAN GET AWAY WITH ANYTHING!

CALVIN! WHAT ON EARTH ARE YOU DOING IN THE COOKIE JAR WITHOUT YOUR CLOTHES ON?!?

YOUR POLLS ARE SLIPPING, DAD. BETTER GET WITH IT.

CALVIN, BEING YOUR DAD IS NOT AN ELECTED POSITION. I DON'T HAVE TO RESPOND TO POLLS.

NOT ELECTED? YOU MEAN YOU CAN GOVERN WITH DICTATORIAL IMPUNITY?

EXACTLY.

IN SHORT, OPEN REVOLT AND EXILE IS THE ONLY HOPE FOR CHANGE?

I DON'T LIKE THE DIRECTION THIS CONVERSATION IS TAKING.

CalViN and HobbES
by WATTERSON

Calvin and Hobbes
by Watterson

I DON'T KNOW.

DO YOU THINK BOOGEYMEN REALLY EXIST?

...BUT IF THEY DO, I'M SURE THIS IS WHERE THEY LIVE.

THAT WAS THE CREEPIEST CAMPFIRE STORY I'VE EVER HEARD. LET'S GET BACK TO THE TENT!

I DON'T THINK I'LL EVER SLEEP AGAIN.

SHH!

WHAT? DID YOU HEAR SOMETHING??

DIDN'T YOU?

I DON'T KNOW. WHAT DID IT SOUND LIKE?

SORT OF LIKE BREATHING AND DROOLING AND RIPPING THE MEAT OFF HUMAN BONES.

YAAHHHH

YOU WERE RIGHT. I'M *GLAD* WE CARRIED A GENERATOR ALL THIS DISTANCE.

WATTERSON

HEY, MOM, CAN WE GO OUT FOR PIZZA TONIGHT?

NO, WE HAD PIZZA LAST NIGHT, AND BESIDES, IT'S TOO EXPENSIVE TO EAT OUT ALL THE TIME.

OH, YOU'D RATHER BLOW THE EVENING COOKING AND WASHING DISHES THAN SPEND A FEW BUCKS?

IT SEEMS LIKE WE GO OUT FOR PIZZA A LOT THESE DAYS.

IF YOU'D RATHER FIX A DISH OF CEREAL AT HOME, BE MY GUEST.

HOBBES WANTS TRIPLE ANCHOVIES.

CALVIN AND HIS TRUSTY NAVIGATOR HOBBES ROAR DOWN THE RESIDENTIAL ROAD AT 90 M.P.H.!

HOBBES PUTS ON THE TURN SIGNAL.

FASTER AND FASTER THEY GO! A BUSLOAD OF SCHOOLCHILDREN DIVES FROM THE SIDEWALK!

HOBBES PUTS ON THE WINDSHIELD WIPERS.

THE POLICE ARE AFTER THEM! CALVIN CRAWLS DOWN TO PUT IN THE CLUTCH AND SHIFT!

HOBBES STEERS AND BLOWS THE HORN!

ALL RIGHT, I'M BACK ALREADY! CAN'T I EVEN RUN AN ERRAND WITHOUT YOU BLOWING THE HORN ACROSS THE PARKING LOT?!

IT WAS HOBBES, MOM. NOT ME.

SEE ANY UFOs?

NOT YET.

WELL, KEEP YOUR EYES PEELED. THEY'RE BOUND TO LAND HERE SOONER OR LATER.

WHAT WILL WE DO WHEN THEY COME?

SEE IF WE CAN SELL MOM AND DAD INTO SLAVERY FOR A STAR CRUISER.

146

149

Calvin and Hobbes

by WATTERSON

QUIT SQUIRMING, CALVIN. YOU'VE GOT ICE CREAM ALL OVER YOUR SHIRT.

RATS, I WAS SAVING IT FOR LATER.

THANKS FOR THE ICE CREAM, DAD. IT WAS GREAT.

YOU'RE WELCOME.

I'M TIRED OF PULLING YOU. IT'S *MY* TURN TO RIDE.

YOUR DAD DIDN'T GET ME ANY ICE CREAM, SO I GET TO RIDE BOTH WAYS.

NO, YOU DON'T! DAD SAID TIGERS DON'T *LIKE* ICE CREAM! IT'S MY TURN TO RIDE.!

TIGERS DON'T KNOW IF THEY LIKE ICE CREAM UNTIL THEY TRY EVERY KIND. I'M NOT PULLING.

I'VE GOT NEWS, FUZZ BRAIN. I'M NOT PULLING, EITHER!

WELL THEN, I GUESS WE'LL BOTH JUST SIT HERE UNTIL WE DIE.

WHY DO THESE "WALKS" ALWAYS END UP AS "RIDES"?

OH, YOU NEED THE EXERCISE MORE ANYWAY.

153

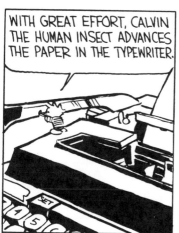

WITH GREAT EFFORT, CALVIN THE HUMAN INSECT ADVANCES THE PAPER IN THE TYPEWRITER.

HIS ONLY HOPE FOR PROPER MEDICAL TREATMENT LIES IN HIS ABILITY TO WRITE A LEGIBLE MESSAGE TO HIS FAMILY!

HE CRAWLS TO EACH KEY AND JUMPS!

WHO WROTE "HELP I'M A BUG" ON MY LETTER TO GRANDMA?

EVIDENTLY SOME BUG. HOW STRANGE.

BACK AND FORTH.

BACK AND FORTH.

TIDAL WAVE!

BEATS ME, MOM. MAYBE THE SEAL AROUND THE TUB LEAKS.

WHAT'S THIS MUSIC?

IT'S "THE 1812 OVERTURE."

I KINDA LIKE IT. INTERESTING PERCUSSION SECTION.

THOSE ARE CANNONS.

AND THEY PERFORM THIS IN CROWDED CONCERT HALLS?? GEE, I THOUGHT CLASSICAL MUSIC WAS BORING!

TOMORROW WE'RE GOING TO DISCUSS "CURRENT EVENTS" IN SCHOOL.

EACH OF US HAS TO FIND A NEWSPAPER ARTICLE, READ IT TO THE CLASS, AND EXPLAIN IT.

WHAT ARTICLE DID YOU CHOOSE?

THIS ONE.

"SPACE ALIEN WEDS TWO-HEADED ELVIS CLONE."

ACTUALLY, THERE'S NOT MUCH LEFT TO EXPLAIN.

LOOK WHAT YOU CAN DO WITH BIG SOCKS!

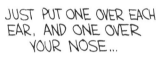

JUST PUT ONE OVER EACH EAR, AND ONE OVER YOUR NOSE...

AN ELEPHANT! HA HA! I WANT SOME SOCKS TOO!

IF I MISS THE BUS, IT'S GOING TO BE UNPLEASANT AROUND HERE!

CALVIN, HOW DID YOU BREAK THIS DISH?!

I WAS CARRYING TOO MUCH AND IT DROPPED.

YOUR PROBLEM IS YOU'VE GOT NO COMMON SENSE.

I'VE GOT **PLENTY** OF COMMON SENSE!

I JUST CHOOSE TO IGNORE IT.

I DON'T UNDERSTAND THIS BUSINESS ABOUT DEATH.

IF WE'RE JUST GOING TO DIE, WHAT'S THE POINT OF LIVING?

WELL, THERE'S SEAFOOD...

I DON'T KNOW WHY I EVEN *TALK* TO YOU BEFORE DINNER.

I'VE DECIDED I WANT TO BE A MILLIONAIRE WHEN I GROW UP.

WELL, YOU'LL HAVE TO WORK PRETTY HARD TO GET A MILLION DOLLARS.

NO, I WON'T. YOU WILL.

ME?

I JUST WANT TO INHERIT IT.

THE WORST PART ABOUT GOING TO SCHOOL IS WAITING FOR THE BUS.

ALL YOU CAN DO IS STAND HERE AND IMAGINE WHAT'S GOING TO GO WRONG DURING THE DAY. I BET WE HAVE A POP MATH QUIZ OR SOMETHING.

WELL, HERE COMES THE BUS. THANKS FOR WAITING WITH ME.

MY PLEASURE.

BOY, MY LUNCH BOX SEEMS LIGHT.

AH... AH... **AH**..

..**AH**...

KBTHCHH!

WHY'D YOU HOLD IT IN?

I'M TRYING TO BLOW MY SHOES OFF.

IT SAYS ON THE BACK OF THIS RECORD THAT THE COMPOSER COULD PLAY THE PIANO AT AGE THREE.

HE WROTE HIS FIRST SYMPHONY WHEN HE WAS FOUR.

THAT'S AMAZING.

WHEN I WAS FOUR, I THINK I WAS TOILET TRAINED.

I'M DONE WITH MY HOMEWORK!

I'M GOING OUTSIDE TO PLAY! I'VE GOT MY JACKET!

I'M LEAVING NOW!

...FURTHER BULLETINS AS EVENTS WARRANT!

WE'RE GOING TO CARVE A JACK-O'-LANTERN NOW.

SEE, WE'LL MAKE A FACE ON THIS PUMPKIN SO IT WILL LOOK LIKE A HEAD.

BUT FIRST WE HAVE TO OPEN UP THE TOP AND SCOOP OUT THE GLOP INSIDE.

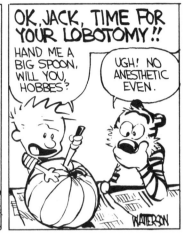

OK, JACK, TIME FOR YOUR LOBOTOMY!! HAND ME A BIG SPOON, WILL YOU, HOBBES?

UGH! NO ANESTHETIC EVEN.

I THINK DAD LIKES HALLOWEEN AS MUCH AS WE DO.

IS HE TAKING US TRICK OR TREATING TONIGHT?

NO, MOM IS.

IS HE GOING TO STAY HOME AND GIVE OUT CANDY?

NO, HE'S GOING TO SIT IN THE BUSHES WITH THE GARDEN HOSE AND DRENCH POTENTIAL T.P.ERS.

OOG, I FEEL AWFUL.

IF SOMEONE EVEN MENTIONS "MILK DUDS," I'M GONNA BARF.

ANOTHER HALLOWEEN COME AND GONE.

IT'S ALWAYS SUCH A LETDOWN AFTER A HOLIDAY.

WE MIGHT AS WELL GO INTO TOWN AND LOOK AT THE CHRISTMAS DECORATIONS.

MOM'S NOT FEELING WELL, SO I'M MAKING HER A "GET WELL" CARD.

THAT'S THOUGHTFUL OF YOU.

SEE, ON THE FRONT IT SAYS, "GET WELL SOON."

AND ON THE INSIDE IT SAYS, "BECAUSE MY BED ISN'T MADE, MY CLOTHES NEED TO BE PUT AWAY, AND I'M HUNGRY."

"LOVE, CALVIN." WANT TO SIGN IT?

SURE. I'M HUNGRY TOO.

WATTERSON

HI, MOM! SINCE YOU'RE SICK, I'M BRINGING YOU BREAKFAST IN BED!

I PREPARED EGGS, TOAST AND ORANGE JUICE FOR YOU ALL BY MYSELF!

HOW NICE!

THE EGGS KIND OF BURNED AND STUCK TO THE PAN, BUT YOU CAN PROBABLY CHIP THEM OUT WITH THIS CHISEL.

UM... WHERE IS THE TOAST AND ORANGE JUICE?

DAD SAID NOT TO TELL YOU ABOUT THAT TILL YOU'RE BETTER.

WATTERSON

SINCE YOUR MOM'S SICK, I'LL BE MAKING DINNER TONIGHT.

YOU CAN COOK?

OF COURSE I CAN COOK.

WATTERSON

AS YOU CAN SEE, I SURVIVED TWO YEARS OF MY OWN COOKING WHEN I HAD AN APARTMENT AFTER COLLEGE.

MOM SAYS YOU ATE FROZEN WAFFLES AND CANNED SOUP THREE MEALS A DAY.

YOUR MOM WASN'T THERE, SO SHE WOULDN'T KNOW. GET THE SYRUP OUT, WILL YOU?

SOMETIMES WHEN *I'M* SICK, YOU READ ME A STORY. WANT ME TO READ *YOU* ONE?

NO, THANKS, CALVIN. I JUST WANT TO REST.

IT'S HARD TO BE A MOM FOR A MOM.

YOU DO FINE, SWEETIE.

WHOA! HEY! ARE YOU CONTAGIOUS??

WHAT'S WRONG WITH YOUR MOM, DO YOU KNOW?

NO. SHE WENT TO THE DOCTOR TODAY, THOUGH.

I WONDER IF... NAH.

WHAT?

YOU DON'T SUPPOSE SHE'S GOING TO HAVE A BABY, DO YOU?

A BABY?!?

WHY WOULD SHE WANT ANOTHER KID?? SHE'S ALREADY GOT *ME!*

YES, YOU'D THINK SHE'D HAVE LEARNED HER LESSON...

I ASKED DAD IF MOM WAS GOING TO HAVE A BABY, AND HE SAID NOT THAT *HE* KNEW OF.

DAD SAID WE'D KNOW IF MOM WAS HAVING A KID BECAUSE SHE'D LOOK LIKE A HIPPOPOTAMUS WITH A GLAND PROBLEM.

...THAT'S WHEN MOM CREAMED HIM WITH HER PILLOW.

DAD SAYS SHE MUST BE FEELING BETTER.

YOU HAVE WEIRD PARENTS.

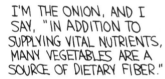

I'VE GOT IT ALL FIGURED OUT, HOBBES. THIS PLAY WILL BE NO SWEAT.

YOU HAVE YOUR LINE ALL MEMORIZED?

NO, I THOUGHT I'D COME OUT, DO A LITTLE SOFT-SHOE, AND AD-LIB SOMETHING!

AD-LIB SOMETHING ABOUT DIETARY FIBER?

EITHER THAT, OR I'LL DO MY ONION IN MIME!

HOW'S MY ONION COSTUME COMING, MOM?

I'M STILL WORKING ON IT. I WISH YOUR CLASS WOULD DO SOMETHING A LITTLE LESS ELABORATE. I'M NOT MUCH OF A SEAMSTRESS.

JUST BE GLAD I'M NOT RUSSY WHITE. *HE* HAS TO BE AN AMINO ACID.

MM... WHAT DO YOU THINK?

JABBA THE HUTT MEETS RUDOLF THE REINDEER. I DUNNO, MOM.

ARE YOU GOING TO COME TO MY PLAY, DAD? IT'S CALLED "NUTRITION AND THE FOUR FOOD GROUPS."

I'LL PROBABLY HAVE TO BE AT WORK, CALVIN.

BUT DAD, IT'LL BE GREAT DRAMA! I'M AN ONION!

WELL, WHY DON'T YOU SAY YOUR LINE FOR ME NOW?

OK! UM... ..LET'S SEE.. "IN ADDITION TO..." ..UH... HOLD IT... UM..

25 KIDS IN FOOD SUITS, FORGETTING THEIR LINES. I'LL *DEFINITELY* BE AT WORK.

DEAR! CALVIN'S WORKED HARD.

OK, UH... "IN ADDITION.." ..UH NO, WAIT.. UM...

DO YOU HAVE YOUR LINE MEMORIZED FOR THE NUTRITION PLAY, CALVIN?

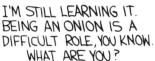
I'M STILL LEARNING IT. BEING AN ONION IS A DIFFICULT ROLE, YOU KNOW. WHAT ARE YOU?

I'M "FAT."

NO, I MEAN IN THE PLAY.

ANYONE *ELSE* WANT TO SAY IT ?!?

AACKK! UNDERSTUDY! UNDERSTUDY!

THANKS FOR WAITING FOR THE BUS WITH ME, HOBBES. I FEEL LIKE AN IDIOT IN THIS ONION SUIT.

I'LL BE GLAD WHEN THIS STUPID PLAY IS OVER.

OH NO! RUN FOR YOUR LIFE! A PRODUCE TRUCK!

...JUST KIDDING!

SUSIE, WHERE'S CALVIN? HE GOES ONSTAGE RIGHT AFTER YOU!

I DON'T KNOW, MISS WORMWOOD. HE WAS HERE A MINUTE AGO.

MAYBE HE WENT TO THE BOYS' ROOM.

HE'S ON IN TWO MINUTES! FINE TIME TO GO TO THE BOYS' ROOM!

FINE TIME TO GET STUCK IN MY COSTUME. STUPID ZIPPER!

Calvin and Hobbes

by WATTERSON

OP ZIP ZOP ZIP ZOP ZIP ZOP ZIP ZOP ZIP ZOP ZIP ZOP ZIP ZOP

SNOW PANTS.

WELL? LET'S HAVE SOME SNOW!!

IT'S SNOWING! I CAN MAKE IT SNOW! I'M PSYCHOKINETIC! HEY! HEY!

OOH, HE'S GOING TO HATE ME FOR THIS.

WANT TO TRADE SANDWICHES, CALVIN?

NO, I'VE GOT MY FAVORITE KIND. WHAT DID YOU BRING?

PEANUT BUTTER.

I HAVE PROCESSED MOUSE LOAF.

OH, GROSS. THAT'S NOT REALLY MOUSE LOAF. IT LOOKS LIKE EGG SALAD.

TASTE IT AND SEE. HERE, I THINK THIS IS A WHISKER. IT'S GOOD.

FORGET IT. I DON'T EVEN WANT MY *OWN* LUNCH ANY MORE.

YOU DON'T? WHAT KIND OF COOKIES ARE THOSE?

TRIP!

TA-DAAA!!

HOW DO THEY KNOW THE LOAD LIMIT ON BRIDGES, DAD?

LOAD LIMIT 10 TONS

THEY DRIVE BIGGER AND BIGGER TRUCKS OVER THE BRIDGE UNTIL IT BREAKS.

THEN THEY WEIGH THE LAST TRUCK AND REBUILD THE BRIDGE.

OH. I SHOULD'VE GUESSED.

DEAR, IF YOU DON'T KNOW THE ANSWER, JUST TELL HIM!

IT'S HARD TO BELIEVE PEOPLE STILL STARVE IN THIS WORLD.

THERE'S EVEN HUNGER IN AMERICA.

WATTERSON

SOME PEOPLE NEVER GET ENOUGH TO EAT.

BOY, I KNOW WHAT *THAT'S* LIKE!

NO YOU DON'T.

THE SOLDIERS ADVANCE UP THE HILL!

OH, NO! A SQUADRON OF BOMBERS APPEARS ON THE HORIZON! THE BOMBS BEGIN TO FALL!

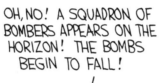

BONK BONK

TWO DIRECT HITS!

I SEE YOU UP THERE!

WATTERSON

LOOK, HOBBES, YOU GET A PLASTIC TRINKET IN BOXES OF "CHOCOLATE-FROSTED SUGAR BOMBS"!

IT SAYS, "BE THE FIRST IN YOUR NEIGHBORHOOD TO COLLECT ALL TEN COLORS."

YEAH, BUT MOM SAYS SHE WON'T BUY ANY MORE CEREAL UNTIL THIS BOX IS GONE.

THAT SHOULDN'T TAKE MORE THAN A COUPLE HOURS, RIGHT?

I DUNNO. AFTER FIVE BOWLS, I GET PRETTY WIRED.

WATTERSON

179

CALVIN, YOUR DAD AND I ARE GOING OUT TOMORROW, SO YOU'LL BE HAVING A BABY SITTER.

OH NO! NOT ROSALYN!

I CALLED EIGHT PEOPLE AND SHE'S THE ONLY ONE WHO WOULD DO IT.

CALL SOME MORE! CALL SOME MORE!

CALVIN, I SPENT AN HOUR ON THE PHONE ALREADY. ROSALYN'S FINE.

"FINE"?? SHE'S A BARRACUDA IN A HIGH SCHOOL SENIOR SUIT! I'M AS GOOD AS DEAD!

YOU REMEMBER AMY? SHE JUST LAUGHED WHEN I CALLED HER.

OH NO! A KNOCK AT THE DOOR! THE BABY SITTER MUST BE HERE!

SHOULD WE HIDE?

NO WAY. BABY SITTERS CAN SMELL FEAR IN LITTLE KIDS. WE'D BE DOOMED.

SO WE GO ON THE OFFENSIVE?

RIGHT. HERE'S A NOTEPAD AND PENCIL.

OH BOY, BLACKMAIL!

RIGHT. GET TO THE UPSTAIRS PHONE WHEN SHE CALLS HER BOYFRIEND.

WE'RE GOING, ROSALYN. HELP YOURSELF TO ANYTHING IN THE FRIDGE.

OK, GOOD-BYE.

CALVIN? ARE YOU UPSTAIRS?

WAP WAP

ALL RIGHT, KID! BEDTIME FOR BONZO!!

WHAT?! GET AWAY! IT'S NOT EVEN 6 O'CLOCK!

A BRILLIANT BOLT OF DEADLY FRAP RAY BLAZES BY THE INTREPID SPACEMAN SPIFF!

OUR HERO HAS VERY HIGH INSURANCE PREMIUMS.

THE COURAGEOUS SPACEMAN SPIFF IS HIT! HE PLUMMETS TOWARD PLANET ZOG!

BREAKING THROUGH THE CLOUD LAYER, HE CAREENS OVER AN ALIEN CITY! THERE'S NO PLACE TO LAND!

SPIFF WRESTLES THE UNCOOPERATIVE CONTROLS! MORE FREEM DRIVE TO THE THRUSTER BLASTERS!

TOO MUCH STRESS! THE FUEL EXPLODES IN FLAME!

THE SITUATION IS GRIM! TEN SECONDS TO IMPACT! NINE .... EIGHT...

WELL, CALVIN??

SEVEN!

VERY GOOD, CALVIN. TEN MINUS THREE EQUALS SEVEN. I DIDN'T THINK YOU WERE PAYING ATTENTION. THAT QUESTION WAS WORTH THREE POINTS.

OUR HERO MIRACULOUSLY MAKES A THREE-POINT LANDING. SPIFF SAVES THE DAY AGAIN!

WHAT A ROTTEN DAY.

ZZ...MMP.. BGZ..

AHHHH...

GNZ.. HEE HEE ZZZ..

FUZZ THERAPY.

ZZZ.. NUK NUK WOONK..

HELLO SUSIE, THIS IS CALVIN. I LOST OUR HOMEWORK ASSIGNMENT. CAN YOU TELL ME WHAT WE WERE SUPPOSED TO READ FOR TOMORROW?

ARE YOU SURE YOU'RE NOT CALLING FOR SOME OTHER REASON?

WHY ELSE WOULD I CALL YOU?

MAYBE YOU MISSED THE MELODIOUS SOUND OF MY VOICE.

WHAT ARE YOU, CRAZY?? ALL I WANT IS THE STUPID ASSIGNMENT!

FIRST SAY YOU MISSED THE MELODIOUS SOUND OF MY VOICE.

THIS IS BLACKMAIL!

I'M HOME FROM SCHOOL!

OOF!

HELLOO

BONK BING BOING

HOW'S *THAT* FOR AN ENTHUSIASTIC GREETING??

SOMETIMES I WISH YOU'D JUST BUY ME ONE OF THOSE "I MISSED YOU" CARDS.

I'VE GOT A GREAT IDEA FOR SCHOOL TOMORROW.

I CUT A PING-PONG BALL IN HALF, AND NOW I'M DRAWING DOTS ON EACH END.

I'LL JUST PUT ONE OVER EACH EYE, AND IT WILL LOOK LIKE I'M REALLY PAYING ATTENTION.

...OR WILL I LOOK *TOO* INTERESTED?

I DOUBT IT. I'M OVER HERE.

WATTERSON

BAD NEWS ON YOUR POLLS, DAD.

YOU SLIPPED ANOTHER TWO NOTCHES. THINGS ARE LOOKING GRIM FOR FUTURE OFFICE.

IS THAT SO?

ANY IDEAS ON WHAT WOULD IMPROVE MY STANDINGS?

I NEED A VCR.

RIGHT. I'LL KEEP THAT IN MIND.

I HOPE YOU'RE READING THE "HELP WANTED" SECTION.

WATTERSON

LOOK, I GOT A LETTER I'M SUPPOSED TO COPY AND SEND TO 20 PEOPLE FOR GOOD LUCK.

IT'S A CHAIN LETTER.

IT SAYS, "A MAN IN DENVER MADE 20 COPIES AND THE NEXT DAY HE GOT A RAISE. A MAN IN SEATTLE BROKE THE CHAIN AND HE WENT BALD!"

WATTERSON

HA! YOU BELIEVE THAT? THESE LETTERS ARE FOR SUPERSTITIOUS NINCOMPOOPS. THROW IT AWAY.

"...AND A DUMB KID LIKE YOU LISTENED TO A FRIEND AND GOT RUN OVER BY A CEMENT MIXER."

Calvin and Hobbes
by WATTERSON

I'M READY FOR BED, DAD. WHAT'S TONIGHT'S STORY GOING TO BE?

HERE'S ONE. "READINGS ON DIALECTICAL METAPHYSICS." YOU'LL LOVE IT.

FORGET IT, DAD. YOU CAN'T GET ME TO DROP OFF *THAT* EASY.

WILL YOU READ US *THIS* STORY? HOBBES WROTE IT HIMSELF.

HOBBES WROTE IT, HUH?

"GOLDILOCKS AND THE THREE TIGERS."

OH BOY, THIS IS GONNA BE GREAT!

"ONCE UPON A TIME THERE LIVED A YOUNG GIRL NAMED GOLDILOCKS. SHE WENT INTO THE FOREST AND SAW A COTTAGE. NO ONE WAS HOME SO SHE WENT IN."

"INSIDE SHE SAW THREE BOWLS OF PORRIDGE. A BIG BOWL, A MEDIUM BOWL, AND A SMALL BOWL. SHE WAS JUST ABOUT TO TASTE THE PORRIDGE WHEN THE THREE TIGERS CAME HOME."

"THEY QUICKLY DIVIDED GOLDILOCKS INTO BIG, MEDIUM, AND SMALL PIECES AND DUNKED THEM IN THE PORRIDGE THAT..."

CALVIN, I'M NOT GOING TO FINISH THIS! THIS IS DISGUSTING!!

I DON'T KNOW WHY I LET YOU TALK ME INTO THIS. *GOOD NIGHT!*

CLICK

HE DIDN'T EVEN LOOK AT OUR ILLUSTRATIONS.

NOW I'M ALL HUNGRY.

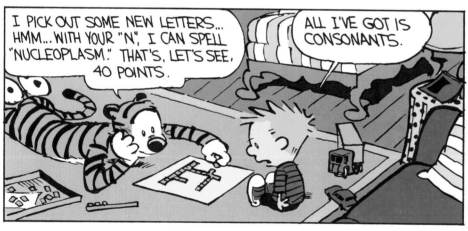

CALVIN HAS MYSTERIOUSLY SHRUNK TO THE SIZE OF AN INSECT!

HIS ONLY HOPE IS TO CALL FOR HELP! PUSHING WITH ALL HIS MIGHT, CALVIN DIALS THE GIGANTIC TELEPHONE!

DEF 3   ABC 2

IT'S RINGING! HE RUNS TO THE MOUTHPIECE! WILL ANYONE BE ABLE TO HEAR HIM??

BZZ BZ! BZZZZ! BZZ BZZ! BZZZ BZ!

CALVIN, THIS HAD BETTER NOT BE YOU.

WATTERSON

FWOOSHHH

GREETINGS, EARTH FEMALE. DO NOT BE ALARMED.

OUR PLANET IS DYING. WE NEED COOKIES TO SURVIVE. DO NOT TRY TO RESIST OR YOU WILL BE DESTROYED.

WE'LL SEE ABOUT THAT. GET BACK HERE.

WHY DO I HAVE TO GO TO BED NOW? I NEVER GET TO DO WHAT I WANT!

IF I GROW UP TO BE SOME SORT OF PSYCHOPATH BECAUSE OF THIS, YOU'LL ALL BE SORRY!!

WATTERSON

NOBODY EVER BECAME A PSYCHOPATH BECAUSE HE HAD TO GO TO BED AT A REASONABLE HOUR.

YEAH, BUT YOU WON'T LET ME CHEW TOBACCO EITHER! YOU NEVER KNOW WHAT MIGHT PUSH ME OVER THE BRINK!

GO TO BED, CALVIN.

190

PSST! ARE YOU AWAKE?

IS IT CHRISTMAS? IT IS! IT IS!

LET'S GO WAKE MOM AND DAD AND OPEN ALL OUR LOOT!

SINCE IT'S CHRISTMAS, MAYBE WE SHOULD LET THEM SLEEP IN A LITTLE.

THAT'S LONG ENOUGH! WAKE UP! WAKE UP! IT'S CHRISTMAS!

QUARTER TO 6. HE LET US SLEEP IN THIS YEAR.

OMIGOSH! THIS LIBRARY BOOK WAS DUE TWO DAYS AGO!

WHAT WILL THEY DO? ARE THEY GOING TO INTERROGATE ME AND BEAT ME UP?! ARE THEY GOING TO BREAK MY KNEES?? WILL I HAVE TO SIGN SOME CONFESSION???

THEY'LL FINE YOU TEN CENTS. NOW GO RETURN IT.

THE WAY SOME OF THOSE LIBRARIANS LOOK AT YOU, I NATURALLY ASSUMED THE CONSEQUENCES WOULD BE MORE DIRE.

HEY DAD, I HAVE A QUESTION.

SURE, CALVIN. WHAT DO YOU WANT TO KNOW?

IF YOU PLUGGED UP YOUR NOSE AND MOUTH RIGHT BEFORE YOU SNEEZED...

...WOULD THE SNEEZE GO OUT YOUR EARS, OR WOULD YOUR HEAD EXPLODE?

I WAS KIND OF HOPING YOU HAD A MATH PROBLEM OR SOMETHING.

...EITHER WAY, I'M SCARED TO TRY IT.

Calvin and Hobbes

by WATTERSON

TOBOGGANS GIVE BETTER RIDES THAN RUNNER SLEDS.

WHY IS THAT?

THERE'S NO WAY TO STEER.

ON THESE CLOUDY WINTER DAYS, SOMETIMES I LIKE TO LIE BACK ON MY SLED AND LOOK AT THE SKY.

IT'S JUST GRAY AND SILENT. NO BIRDS SINGING OR BUGS BUZZING. EVERYTHING IS MUFFLED BY THE SNOW.

IMAGINE WHAT IT WOULD BE LIKE WITHOUT ANY PEOPLE OR HOUSES AROUND. IT WOULD BE PERFECTLY STILL.

PRETTY NEAT, HUH?

YES, VERY PEACEFUL.

I HATE ALL THAT SILENCE.

BEHOLD THE DREADED TOBOGGAN: SUICIDE SLED.

IT'S UNIQUE DESIGN SENDS A BLINDING SPRAY OF SNOW ON IT'S PASSENGERS AT THE SLIGHTEST BUMP. NOTE, TOO, THE LACK OF ANY STEERING MECHANISM.

YES, THIS SLED IS TRULY A HAZARD TO LIFE AND LIMB.

WHEEE OOMPH! EEEEE

BOY, IS IT COLD! CAN'T WE TURN THE HEAT UP?

HEAT IS EXPENSIVE, CALVIN. JUST PUT ON A SWEATER.

LOOK, THE THERMOSTAT GOES ALL THE WAY UP TO 90 DEGREES! WE COULD BE SITTING AROUND IN OUR SHORTS!

LEAVE THE THERMOSTAT ALONE, CALVIN.

I CAN ALMOST SEE MY BREATH. I'LL JUST CRANK IT UP TO 75, OK?

I SAID DON'T TOUCH IT!

GEE, MY HANDS ARE SO NUMB, I CAN'T MOVE THE SWITCH. GUESS I'LL PUT ON A SWEATER.

OOH, YOU LOOK COLD, CALVIN! THERE'S A FIRE MADE. WHY DON'T YOU GO WARM UP?

OH BOY!

NOTHING BEATS SITTING BY A ROARING FIRE AFTER YOU'VE BEEN OUT IN THE COLD.

OF COURSE, SOME PEOPLE SAY WHY BOTHER GOING OUTSIDE FIRST?

FOR ALL THAT PREPARATION, YOU SURE ARE A LOUSY SHOT!

GO AHEAD DOWN. YOU'LL MISS ALL THOSE TREES.

YOU CAN DO IT. YOU'LL STOP BEFORE YOU GO OVER THAT LEDGE AT THE BOTTOM.

YOU WON'T GO INTO THAT POND. BESIDES, THE ICE IS PROBABLY REAL THICK ANYWAY. GO AHEAD DOWN.

MY BRAIN IS TRYING TO KILL ME.

GALOSH
GALOSH
GALOSH

I CALLED SUSIE A BOOGER-BRAIN AFTER SCHOOL, AND SHE WENT HOME CRYING.

GOODNESS, WHY'D YOU DO *THAT*?

I DUNNO. I WAS JUST TEASING.

IT SOUNDS LIKE YOU HURT HER FEELINGS.

I DIDN'T MEAN FOR HER TO TAKE THE INSULT *PERSONALLY!*

✳SNIFF✳ THAT STUPID CALVIN. WHY DOES HE CALL ME NAMES FOR NO REASON? IT'S JUST MEAN.

I WISH I HAD A HUNDRED FRIENDS. *THEN* I WOULDN'T CARE. I'D SAY, "WHO NEEDS *YOU*, CALVIN? I'VE GOT A HUNDRED OTHER FRIENDS!"

THEN MY HUNDRED FRIENDS AND I WOULD GO DO SOMETHING FUN, AND LEAVE CALVIN ALL ALONE! HA!

...AND AS LONG AS I'M DREAMING, I'D LIKE A PONY.

I FEEL BAD THAT I CALLED SUSIE NAMES AND HURT HER FEELINGS.

I'M SORRY I DID IT.

MAYBE YOU SHOULD APOLOGIZE TO HER.

I KEEP HOPING THERE'S A LESS OBVIOUS SOLUTION.

WELL, WELL! IT'S AN INVITATION TO SUSIE DERKINS' BIRTHDAY PARTY. HOW NICE.

SUSIE INVITED *YOU*? WHAT ABOUT ME? DOES IT SAY ME TOO?

NO, IT DOESN'T SAY ANYTHING ABOUT YOU.

SHE MUST HAVE MAILED MY INVITATION SEPARATELY. SHE PROBABLY WANTED TO INSURE IT SO SHE'LL KNOW IT DIDN'T GET LOST. SOMETIMES THOSE TAKE LONGER.

I'LL HAVE TO SIGN FOR IT AND ALL. I'M SURE SHE'S TAKING NO CHANCES WITH MINE.

OH WAIT. ON THE BACK IT SAYS, "YOU CAN BRING THAT STUPID KID YOU HANG AROUND WITH, IF YOU MUST."

WE GET TO GO TO A BIRTHDAY PARTY!

THAT STUPID SUSIE.

BALLOONS, CAKE, PRESENTS... OH BOY!

SHE WON'T BE GETTING A VERY BIG PRESENT FROM *ME*, THAT'S FOR SURE.

I BET WE'LL PLAY GAMES, TOO! IT WILL BE FUN!

HMPH.

MAYBE WE'LL PLAY "SPIN THE BOTTLE"!

OH GET REAL!

I'LL MAKE A LIST OF POSSIBLE GIFTS FOR SUSIE'S BIRTHDAY. WHAT SHOULD WE GIVE HER?

HOW ABOUT A MOUTH FULL OF BROKEN TEETH? THAT'S WHAT *I'D* LIKE TO GIVE HER.

OH, DON'T BE SO CRANKY.

I THINK WE SHOULD GET HER A CAN OF TUNA FISH.

TUNA FISH? WHY WOULD SHE WANT *THAT*?

WELL, MAYBE SHE WOULDN'T, AND WE COULD OFFER TO TAKE IT BACK..... AND BORROW SOME BREAD, A LITTLE MAYO ...

RIGHT, HOBBES.

SUSIE'S HOUSE IS THE NEXT ONE UP.

THIS IS OUR LAST CHANCE TO NOT SHOW UP AND HAVE A NEW BIKE HORN.

HI, SUSIE. HAPPY BIRTHDAY!

HELLO, CALVIN. THANKS FOR COMING.

OH, LOOK AT YOUR STUFFED TIGER! HE'S WEARING A TIE!

HE'S JUST *ADORABLE!*

OK, YOU WERE RIGHT. GIRLS FLIP FOR TIES. YOU CAN STOP WINKING AT ME.

C'MON IN.

OK, EVERYONE, THE IDEA OF A SCAVENGER HUNT IS TO BRING BACK AS MANY OF THESE ITEMS AS YOU CAN IN HALF AN HOUR. LET'S GO!

QUICK, HOBBES, WHAT'S THE FIRST ITEM?

AN OLD LICENSE PLATE.

GREAT! I SAW ONE ON THE WAY OVER! C'MON!

GOOD THING I ALWAYS CARRY A SWISS ARMY KNIFE. NOBODY'S COMING, RIGHT?

IS THIS GAME LEGAL?

HERE'S A PAPER PLATE FOR THE BIRTHDAY CAKE, CALVIN.

THANK YOU.

I HOPE IT'S GOOD. I HATE IT WHEN THE BIRTHDAY KID CHOOSES SOMETHING GROSS LIKE COCONUT.

YOU DON'T HAVE TO WORRY. IT'S CHOCOLATE.

OH, GOOD. DID YOU SEE IT?

HEY! WHO CUT A PIECE OF MY CAKE ALREADY?! I DIDN'T EVEN GET TO BLOW OUT THE CANDLES!!

IT'S NICE AND MOIST, TOO.

GLAD YOU BOTH COULD COME. THANK YOU FOR THE NICE PRESENT. GOOD-BYE.

MOM MAY NOT WANT THIS PIECE OF CAKE AND ICE CREAM WE'RE BRINGING HER.

HEY! IT SNOWED LAST NIGHT!

OH, BOY! LOOK AT IT ALL! THEY'LL HAVE TO CLOSE THE SCHOOLS!

SNOW EVERYWHERE! IT MUST BE WAIST DEEP!

UNFORTUNATELY, THAT'S A RELATIVE MEASURE.

CAN I HAVE SOME CLAY?

HELP YOURSELF. THIS STUFF'S IMPOSSIBLE TO WORK WITH.

THANKS.

I'VE GOT A PRETTY GOOD BOWL OR SOMETHING GOING HERE.

IT STARTED OUT AS A PHANTOM JET, BUT IT SORT OF SQUASHED, SO NOW I THINK IT'S A BOWL.

MMM. THAT'S VERY GOOD.

YEAH, I'M REAL PLEASED WITH IT.

WATTERSON

UH OH. THERE'S A DINOSAUR IN THE KITCHEN.

YAARRGH

WELL IF YOU SEE CALVIN ANYWHERE, TELL HIM IT'S ALMOST TIME FOR DINNER.

WATTERSON

I'D INVITE YOU, BUT NO DINOSAURS ARE ALLOWED AT THE DINNER TABLE.

HA. DINOSAURS EAT ANYWHERE THEY WANT.

LET'S GO, CALVIN. TIME FOR YOUR BATH.

I'M NOT TAKING BATHS ANYMORE. I HATE THEM.

OH? AND HOW ARE YOU GOING TO STAY CLEAN?

EASY.

WATTERSON

EITHER HE'S PLAYING CLASSICAL MUSIC AT 78 RPM, OR I'M STILL DREAMING.

FIRST THING TOMORROW MORNING, I'M CALLING THE ORPHANAGE.

WHERE DO WE KEEP ALL OUR CHAINSAWS, MOM?

WE DON'T HAVE ANY CHAINSAWS, CALVIN.

WE DON'T? NOT ANY?

NOPE.

HOW AM I EVER GOING TO LEARN HOW TO JUGGLE?

THE GIANT AMOEBA SLIDES ALONG THE KITCHEN FLOOR.

EXTENDING A CYTOPLASMIC PSEUDOPOD, THE PROTOZOAN ENGULFS A PACKAGE OF OATMEAL COOKIES.

CRUNCH CRUNCH

NICE TRY. PUT THEM BACK.

THE MAJESTIC EAGLE CIRCLES SLOWLY IN THE CLOUDS.

WITH EYES SO SHARP HE CAN SPOT MOVEMENT A MILE BELOW, HE SIGHTS HIS PREY AND DIVES!

REACHING SPEEDS OF MORE THAN 100 MPH, HIS UNWARY PRIZE WILL NEVER KNOW WHAT HIT IT!

WAKE UP, DAD! IT'S SATURDAY!

ZZ... WHA?

Calvin and Hobbes

by WATTERSON

HERE IS SUCCESSFUL MR. JONES. HE LIVES IN A 5-ACRE HOME IN A WEALTHY SUBURB. HERE IS HIS NEW MERCEDES IN THE DRIVEWAY.

IT'S ANYONE'S GUESS AS TO HOW MUCH LONGER MR. JONES CAN MEET HIS MONTHLY FINANCE CHARGES.

HERE COMES MR. JONES OUT OF HIS ATTRACTIVE SUBURBAN HOME. HE HOPS IN HIS RED SPORTS CAR.

OFF HE GOES TO WORK. 80...90... 100 MILES AN HOUR!

...ALONG THE EDGE OF THE GRAND CANYON!!

SUDDENLY, HIS STEERING LOCKS AND HIS BRAKES FAIL! HE CAREENS OVER THE EDGE! OH NO! DOWN HE GOES!

HIS ONLY HOPE IS TO CLIMB OUT THE SUN ROOF AND JUMP! MAYBE, JUST MAYBE, HE CAN GRAB A BRANCH AND SAVE HIMSELF! HE UNWINDS THE SUN ROOF! CAN HE MAKE IT??

NO! THE CAR EXPLODES IN MID-AIR, PROPELLING MILLIONS OF TINY SHARDS INTO THE STRATOSPHERE! *KABLOOIE!*

THE NEIGHBORS HEAR THE BOOM ECHOING ACROSS THE CANYON. THEY PILE INTO A MINI-VAN TO INVESTIGATE! WHAT WILL HAPPEN TO *THEM*?

213

calvin and hobbes by WATTERSON

AAAAAHHH! EEEE! HEE HEE HEE HEE! WOO! ACK! HE

216

OH, MOM, I NEED SOME CRISCO FOR SCHOOL TODAY!

SHORTENING? HONESTLY, CALVIN, I WISH YOU'D REMEMBER THESE THINGS THE NIGHT BEFORE. NOW HURRY UP AND GET READY.

RIGHT.

HERE'S THE CRISCO BACK. THANKS.

YOU PUT IT IN YOUR HAIR??

GET BACK HERE! YOU'RE NOT GOING TO SCHOOL LIKE *THAT*!

AW C'MON, MOM! IT'S CLASS PICTURE DAY!

WHAT'S WITH YOUR HAIR?

I TOLD MOM I'M GETTING MY SCHOOL PICTURE TAKEN TODAY, AND SHE MADE ME COMB OUT THE CRISCO I PUT IN MY HAIR. NOW I LOOK LIKE A MORON.

THAT'S TRUE. YOU DO.

WELL DON'T JUST STAND THERE! THINK OF SOMETHING! WHAT CAN I DO?

THERE. MUCH BETTER!

WHAT'D YOU DO? IS IT COOL? IS IT NEW WAVE? GEE, I WISH I HAD A MIRROR...

THE BUS IS GOING TO BE HERE ANY MINUTE. YOU'RE SURE YOU FIXED MY HAIR SO IT LOOKS OK?

IT LOOKS GREAT. TRY NOT TO MUSS IT UP.

YOU'RE NOT KIDDING ME, ARE YOU? THIS REALLY LOOKS GOOD?

TRUST ME. YOU LOOK LIKE ... LIKE ...

"... ASTRO BOY."

ALL RIGHT! I CAN'T *WAIT* TO GET MY PICTURE TAKEN *NOW*!

CALVIN! WHAT DID YOU DO TO YOUR HAIR?? DON'T YOU KNOW WE HAVE OUR PICTURES TAKEN TODAY?

OF COURSE, SILLY. THAT'S WHY I DID IT. IT'S CRISCO.

DOES YOUR MOM KNOW YOU LOOK LIKE THAT?

SORT OF. HOBBES FIXED ME UP A LITTLE AT THE BUS STOP.

WOW. I WISH I HAD SOME CRISCO.

WAIT TILL MOM SENDS MY PICTURE TO GRANDMA!

OK, KID, SIT UP STRAIGHT ON THE STOOL AND LOOK RIGHT AT ME. THAT'S IT.

ARE YOU READY TO TAKE MY PICTURE? SHOULD I TAKE OFF MY SHIRT NOW?

KID, WHAT ARE...? DON'T TAKE OFF YOUR SHIRT!!

SEE? I PAINTED A FACE ON MY STOMACH.

KID, PUT YOUR SHIRT BACK ON.

BUT LOOK! WHEN I BREATHE OUT, THE FACE CHANGES! SEE? OK, TAKE ONE QUICK!

LOOK, HOBBES, I GOT MY SCHOOL PICTURES BACK.

LOOK AT YOU! HA HA HA! LOOK AT YOUR HAIR! HEE HEE! THESE ARE GREAT!

AREN'T THEY, THOUGH?

HEE HEE HEE! LOOK AT THIS ONE! WHAT AN EXPRESSION! HOO HOO HOO! HA HA!

YEAH, SEE HOW I GOT MY ONE EYE TO ROLL BACK?

HA HA HA! YOUR MOTHER'S GOING TO GO INTO CONNIPTIONS, OF COURSE..

OH, C'MON. YEARS FROM NOW, THINK OF THE MEMORIES THESE WILL BRING.

CalViN and HobbEs

by WATTERSON

GLIK
GLIK
GLIK

OH NO! WHAT HAVE
I DONE?!?

THE HUMAN BODY IS 80%
WATER. LITTLE DID CALVIN
REALIZE HOW CRITICAL IT
IS TO MAINTAIN THAT!

NOW IT'S TOO LATE! BY DRINKING THAT
EXTRA GLASS OF WATER, CALVIN HAS
UPSET THAT PRECIOUS BALANCE! HE
IS NOW **90%** WATER!

EVERYTHING SOLID IN CALVIN'S
BODY BEGINS TO DISSOLVE!

HE IS BECOMING
A LIQUID!!

HIS ONLY HOPE IS SOMEHOW TO
GET TO AN ICEBOX AND FREEZE
HIMSELF SOLID UNTIL HE CAN
GET PROPER MEDICAL ATTENTION!

UNFORTUNATELY, AS A LIQUID, CALVIN CAN
ONLY RUN DOWNHILL! CAN HE MAKE IT?
CAN HE MAKE IT??

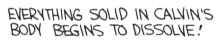

I DON'T THINK I'M
GONNA MAKE IT.

THERE'S A GAS
STATION UP AHEAD.
JUST HOLD ON.

DIDN'T I TELL
YOU NOT TO
DRINK SO MUCH
BEFORE WE
LEFT?!

Calvin and Hobbes

by WATTERSON

HOBBES, LOOK! THERE'S A LITTLE RACCOON ON THE GROUND.

IS IT ALIVE?

I THINK SO, BUT HE'S HURT. SEE, HE'S HARDLY BREATHING.

BETTER NOT TOUCH HIM IF HE'S HURT.

YEAH. YOU WAIT HERE AND GUARD HIM. I'LL RUN AND GET MOM.

I SURE HOPE SHE CAN HELP.

OF COURSE SHE CAN! YOU DON'T GET TO BE MOM IF YOU CAN'T FIX EVERYTHING JUST RIGHT.

THERE'S HOBBES GUARDING HIM, MOM. THE LITTLE RACCOON'S RIGHT OVER THERE!

OOH, CALVIN, I DON'T KNOW IF WE CAN SAVE HIM. HE LOOKS PRETTY BAD. GO GET A SHOE BOX AND A CLEAN DISH TOWEL.

RIGHT!

I DON'T THINK THIS POOR LITTLE GUY IS GOING TO MAKE IT, HOBBES. (SIGH) I HATE IT WHEN THESE THINGS HAPPEN.

...YOU CAN TELL I'M UPSET WHEN I START TALKING TO *YOU*...

WELL, I GOT HIM IN THE SHOE BOX. I GUESS ALL WE CAN DO IS KEEP HIM WARM AND SAFE.

WE'LL KEEP HIM IN THE GARAGE, AND PUT OUT SOME WATER AND FOOD.

I READ IN A BOOK THAT RACCOONS WILL EAT JUST ABOUT ANYTHING.

CHANCES ARE, I'LL BE HAPPY TO DONATE MOST OF MY DINNER.

CALVIN, YOU DON'T EVEN KNOW WHAT WE'RE HAVING.

THIS IS WHERE DAD BURIED THE LITTLE RACCOON.

I DIDN'T EVEN KNOW HE EXISTED A FEW DAYS AGO AND NOW HE'S GONE FOREVER. IT'S LIKE I FOUND HIM FOR NO REASON. I HAD TO SAY GOOD-BYE AS SOON AS I SAID HELLO.

STILL... IN A SAD, AWFUL, TERRIBLE WAY, I'M HAPPY I MET HIM.

SNIFF

WHAT A STUPID WORLD.

YOU KNOW, HOBBES, I CAN'T FIGURE OUT THIS DEATH STUFF.

WHY DID THAT LITTLE RACCOON HAVE TO DIE? HE DIDN'T DO ANYTHING WRONG.

HE WAS JUST LITTLE! WHAT'S THE POINT OF PUTTING HIM HERE AND TAKING HIM BACK SO SOON?!?

IT'S EITHER MEAN OR IT'S ARBITRARY, AND EITHER WAY I'VE GOT THE HEEBIE-JEEBIES.

WHY IS IT ALWAYS NIGHT WHEN WE TALK ABOUT THESE THINGS?

MOM SAYS DEATH IS AS NATURAL AS BIRTH, AND IT'S ALL PART OF THE LIFE CYCLE.

SHE SAYS WE DON'T REALLY UNDERSTAND IT, BUT THERE ARE MANY THINGS WE DON'T UNDERSTAND, AND WE JUST HAVE TO DO THE BEST WE CAN WITH THE KNOWLEDGE WE HAVE.

I GUESS THAT MAKES SENSE.

...BUT DON'T *YOU* GO ANYWHERE.

DON'T WORRY.

HEY! WHAT HAPPENED TO THE TREES HERE? WHO CLEARED OUT THE WOODS?

THERE USED TO BE LOTS OF ANIMALS IN THESE WOODS! NOW IT'S A MUD PIT!

THIS SIGN SAYS, "FUTURE SITE OF SHADY ACRES CONDOMINIUMS."

ANIMALS CAN'T AFFORD CONDOS!

"SHADY ACRES"? THE ONLY SHADE *I* SEE IS FROM THAT BULLDOZER.

WHERE ARE ALL THE ANIMALS SUPPOSED TO LIVE NOW THAT THEY CUT DOWN THESE WOODS TO PUT IN HOUSES??

BY GOLLY, HOW WOULD *PEOPLE* LIKE IT IF ANIMALS BULLDOZED A SUBURB AND PUT IN NEW *TREES*?!?

NO GOOD. THEY DIDN'T LEAVE THE KEYS.

IT TOOK HUNDREDS OF YEARS FOR THESE WOODS TO GROW, AND THEY LEVELED IT IN A WEEK. IT'S GONE.

AFTER THEY BUILD NEW HOUSES HERE, THEY'LL HAVE TO WIDEN THE ROADS AND PUT UP GAS STATIONS, AND PRETTY SOON THIS WHOLE AREA WILL JUST BE A BIG STRIP.

EVENTUALLY THERE WON'T BE A NICE SPOT LEFT ANYWHERE.

I WONDER IF YOU CAN REFUSE TO INHERIT THE WORLD.

I THINK IF YOU'RE BORN, IT'S TOO LATE.

CALVIN and HOBBES

by WATTERSON

Look, Jane. See Spot.
See Spot run.
Run, Spot, run.
Jane sees Spot run.

WAY TO GO, JANE!

BOY, I HATE HOMEWORK.

YAHH! WHOOP! HEY!

YOW! WHOA! STOP!

GALOOP GALOOP

AAAUGHH!!

GAACKK! HELP! HELP!

WHAP!!

BONK! BONK!

WHAT ON EARTH ARE YOU *DOING*? WHERE'S YOUR HOMEWORK?

I COULDN'T CONCENTRATE.

RRINNGGG!

RECESS IS OVER!

R-R-RIPP!

SNAG

OH NO!

WHY IS IT YOU ALWAYS RIP YOUR PANTS ON THE DAY EVERYONE HAS TO DEMONSTRATE A MATH PROBLEM AT THE CHALKBOARD?

WATTERSON

I CAN'T BELIEVE I RIPPED MY PANTS! RECESS IS OVER. I'M SUPPOSED TO BE BACK IN CLASS!

I CAN'T GO IN LIKE THIS! WHAT AM I GOING TO DO??

...OF ALL THE DAYS TO WEAR THE UNDERPANTS WITH THE LITTLE ROCKET SHIPS...

WATTERSON

LOOK AT THE SIZE OF THIS RIP! MAYBE I CAN PULL MY SHIRT DOWN OVER IT.

NO, THAT DOESN'T WORK. MAYBE I CAN TUCK MY SHIRT INTO THE HOLE. ..NOPE..

MAYBE I CAN STICK THE RIPPED PART UNDER MY BELT. NO, THAT DOESN'T WORK EITHER.

WATTERSON

MAYBE I CAN SCOOT AROUND ON MY REAR THE REST OF THE DAY.

CALVIN and HOBBES
by WATTERSON

"DURING EMERGENCY LANDING, REPLACE DINNER TRAY AND BRING SEAT TO UPRIGHT POSITION. EXTINGUISH ALL SMOKING MATERIALS."

"...INCLUDING SPACECRAFT, IF POSSIBLE."

OUT OF FUEL, THE COURAGEOUS SPACEMAN SPIFF IS FORCED TO LAND ON THE DISTANT PLANET ZOK!

THE VALIANT EXPLORER SURVEYS THE ZOKKIAN LANDSCAPE. WHO KNOWS WHAT DANGERS LIE HIDDEN IN THE CRATERED TERRAIN?

UNDAUNTED, SPIFF SETS OUT TO FIND HELP!

MILES LATER, IT IS EVIDENT THE PLANET IS COMPLETELY UNINHABITED!

OUR HERO IS MAROONED ON A LIFELESS PLANET! ALONE ON AN ALIEN WORLD!

ALONE... ALL ALONE...

DARN IT, WHY DOESN'T ANYONE EVER *TELL* ME WHEN THE LUNCH BELL RINGS?

I'VE GOT TO GIVE A 5-MINUTE ORAL REPORT IN SCHOOL ON THURSDAY.

WE'RE SUPPOSED TO RESEARCH OUR SUBJECT, WRITE IT UP, AND PRESENT IT TO THE CLASS WITH A VISUAL AID.

THAT'S A BIG ASSIGNMENT.

I'LL SAY. I HATE MY TEACHER.

SHE KNOWS WE'LL ALL DO IT ON THE LAST EVENING, BUT SHE GAVE US THREE DAYS TO WORRY ABOUT IT.

WHAT'S THE SUBJECT OF YOUR REPORT?

THE BRAIN.

WHAT DO YOU KNOW ABOUT BRAINS?

WELL, I SAW THIS MOVIE WHERE THEY KEPT THIS GUY'S BRAIN ALIVE IN A TANK OF WATER.

THEN A POWER SURGE MUTATED THE BRAIN, AND IT CRAWLED OUT AND TERRORIZED THE POPULACE.

THAT'S INFORMATIVE.

UNFORTUNATELY FOR MY REPORT, MOM CAUGHT ME, AND I DIDN'T GET TO SEE HOW IT ENDED.

I'VE GOT TO GIVE MY REPORT ON "THE BRAIN" AT SCHOOL TODAY.

SEE MY VISUAL AID? I COOKED SOME NOODLES AND PUT THEM IN A PAPER BAG. DOESN'T THAT LOOK LIKE BRAINS?

UGH.

WELL, I GUESS I'M ALL SET.

DID YOU WRITE YOUR REPORT YET?

NAH. I BORROWED MOM'S POCKET DICTIONARY. I'LL DO IT ON THE BUS.

MY FIVE-MINUTE REPORT IS ON "THE BRAIN."

OF COURSE, IT'S DIFFICULT TO EXPLAIN THE COMPLEXITIES OF THE BRAIN IN JUST FIVE MINUTES, BUT TO BEGIN, THE BRAIN IS PART OF THE CENTRAL NERVOUS SYSTEM.

I'LL PAUSE FOR A FEW MOMENTS, SO YOU ALL CAN FINISH WRITING THAT DOWN.

CALVIN!

POW! JAB! KICK! POW! POW!

RATTATATATTATTA RATTATATTATTA

EEEEEEEEEE

BOOM!

PLEASE, PLEASE, PRETTY PLEASE?

NO. YOU SHOULD'VE SAVED SOME OF YOUR OWN HALLOWEEN CANDY.

HEY, CAN WE CHANGE THE CHANNEL NOW? I WANT TO WATCH SOMETHING ELSE.

MY SHOW'S NOT OVER YET.

AW C'MON! YOU SEE THIS PROGRAM ALL THE TIME! CAN'T WE WATCH MY SHOW FOR ONCE?

NO, I WAS HERE FIRST. PIPE DOWN. THIS IS A GOOD PART.

AARRGHH

I HATE NATIONAL GEOGRAPHIC ANIMAL SPECIALS.

Point A is twice as far from point C as point B is from A. If the distance from point B to point C is 5 inches, how far is point A from point C?

THE LIVING DEAD DON'T *NEED* TO SOLVE WORD PROBLEMS.

CALVIN THE ZOMBIE SEARCHES FOR FOOD.

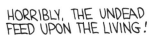

HORRIBLY, THE UNDEAD FEED UPON THE LIVING!

...ALTHOUGH, IN A PINCH, A PBJ WILL DO, IF YOU EAT IT MESSILY ENOUGH.

"WHEN IN ROME..."

I CAN'T GET THIS STUPID HAIR TO COMB RIGHT.

SEE HOW IT STICKS OUT IN BACK?

MAYBE YOU NEED A HAIRCUT.

YEAH, BUT BARBERS NEVER CUT IT THE WAY I WANT.

BOY, WHAT A GREAT IDEA! THANKS!

THIS IS EASY! YOU REALLY THINK YOUR MOM WILL PAY ME EIGHT BUCKS?

SO EXACTLY HOW WOULD YOU LIKE THE BACK CUT?

JUST TRIM THE PART THAT STICKS OUT AND TAPER IT A LITTLE.

WOULDN'T YOU RATHER HAVE IT REAL SHORT?

NO, JUST CUT A LITTLE BIT.

ARE YOU SURE? DON'T YOU THINK IT SHOULD BE REAL SHORT? IT LOOKS LIKE IT SHOULD BE REAL SHORT.

ARE YOU TRYING TO TELL ME SOMETHING?

NO, I JUST THINK IT SHOULD BE REAL SHORT. ESPECIALLY, OH, RIGHT HERE.

YOU MADE A MISTAKE, DIDN'T YOU?

NO. I CAN COVER IT UP.

COVER WHAT UP? WHAT DID YOU DO WRONG?

NOTHING. I CAN'T HELP IT IF YOUR HEAD HAS FUNNY BUMPS THAT MAKE THE SCISSORS GO SCREWY.

YOUR HEAD'S GONNA HAVE "FUNNY BUMPS" IN A MINUTE IF YOU DON'T TELL ME WHAT YOU DID!!

OOPS. HOLD STILL.

WHY'D YOU SAY "OOPS"?! WHAT'D YOU DO NOW?!

NOTHING. LET'S TRY PARTING YOUR HAIR FROM EAR TO EAR.

250

THIS HAIRCUT HAD BETTER LOOK GOOD, FUZZ BRAIN.

YOU'LL LOVE IT. IT'S KIND OF "NEW WAVE."

NEW WAVE? LIKE HOW?

WELL, SORT OF "PUNK," ACTUALLY.

LIKE A MOHAWK?

IN *SOME* PLACES IT'S SORT OF LIKE A MOHAWK.

I WANT A MIRROR.

YOU KNOW WHAT'S THE RAGE THIS YEAR? ...HATS.

LOOK WHAT YOU DID TO MY HAIR! IT LOOKS LIKE IT WAS CUT WITH A WEED-EATER!

NOTHING A LITTLE TONIC AND COMBING CAN'T FIX.

GET AWAY FROM ME, YOU MENACE!

IF MOM SEES THIS, SHE'LL BLOW HER BLOOD VESSELS! WHAT AM I GOING TO DO??

HOW'S THAT? SORT OF THE "LAWRENCE OF ARABIA" LOOK!

SORT OF THE "LOBOTOMY PATIENT" LOOK.

MY CIGARETTE SMOKE MIXED WITH THE SMOKE OF MY .38. IF BUSINESS WAS AS GOOD AS MY AIM, I'D BE ON EASY STREET. INSTEAD, I'VE GOT AN OFFICE ON 49TH STREET AND A NASTY RELATIONSHIP WITH A STRING OF COLLECTION AGENTS.

YEAH, THAT'S ME, TRACER BULLET. I'VE GOT EIGHT SLUGS IN ME. ONE'S LEAD, AND THE REST ARE BOURBON. THE DRINK PACKS A WALLOP, AND I PACK A REVOLVER. I'M A PRIVATE EYE.

SUDDENLY MY DOOR SWUNG OPEN, AND IN WALKED TROUBLE. BRUNETTE, AS USUAL.

TAKE YOUR HAT OFF AT THE DINNER TABLE, CALVIN. IT'S NOT POLITE.

SHE WAS A PUSHY DAME, BUT SHE HAD A CASE..

CalviN and HobbeS

by WATTERSON

THIS IS SUPPOSED TO BE GREAT ART.

...SO WHY DOES IT LOOK LIKE A BUNCH OF DECAPITATED NAKED PEOPLE?

A STRANGE FEELING COMES OVER CALVIN IN THE ART MUSEUM.

HIS PARENTS, ENGROSSED IN CULTURE, REMAIN BLISSFULLY UNAWARE OF CALVIN'S TERRIBLE TRANSFORMATION!

YES, A TYRANNOSAURUS IS LOOSE IN THE ART MUSEUM! THE CURATOR SHRIEKS, AND PANDEMONIUM ENSUES!

A GUARD REACHES FOR HIS PISTOL, BUT THE DINOSAUR IS UPON HIM AND HE IS MESSILY DEVOURED!

THE GIANT LIZARD'S GLORY IS CAPTURED FOREVER ON FILM BY THE ANTI-THEFT CAMERAS! PATRONS OF THE ARTS FLEE FOR THEIR LIVES!

HUNDREDS OF PRICELESS PAINTINGS ARE RIPPED TO SHREDS IN THE AWFUL RAMPAGE! WEALTHY BENEFACTORS ARE TRAMPLED! THE MUSEUM IS IN RUINS! ON TO SYMPHONY HALL!!

CALVIN? ... CALVIN? WE'RE IN THE NEXT ROOM NOW. C'MON.

I THINK WE'D BETTER GET HIM OUT OF HERE. HE HAD THAT GRIN AGAIN.

I WANNA SEE THE DINOSAURS AT THE NATURAL HISTORY MUSEUM AGAIN.

WE SPENT ALL AFTERNOON THERE, CALVIN.

The End